Old Gelligaer

including

Pen-y-bryn, Pen-pedair-heol, Cascade & Glyn-gaer

in Photographs

by Maldwyn Griffiths and Richard Herold

Foreword by
Keith Derrick

Volume 1

Old Bakehouse Publications

Abertillery

First published in October 2002

ISBN 1 874538 79 4

Published in the U.K. by
Old Bakehouse Publications
Church Street,
Abertillery, Gwent NP13 1EA
Telephone: 01495 212600 Fax: 01495 216222
http:/www.mediamaster.co.uk/oldbakebooks

Made and printed in the UK
by J.R. Davies (Printers) Ltd.

British Library Cataloguing in Publication Data: a catalogue
record for this book is available from the British Library.

Foreword

by Keith Derrick
Caerphilly Borough County Councillor and Gelligaer Community Councillor

Born and bred in Penpedairheol, it is with enormous pride that I write this foreword for this excellent book.

To me the name Gelligaer - *'The Grove of the Fort'*, evokes images of Roman soldiers marching across the ridges of the Rhymney Valley. Indeed, in a field behind the ancient church of St. Catwg's, lie the remains of what the renowned archaeologist Sir Mortimer Wheeler once described as *'one of the outstanding examples of a Roman fort in Europe'*.

Beyond this, the history of Gelligaer and its neighbouring villages of Cascade, Glyn-Gaer, Penpedairheol and Penybryn stretches across thousands of years. From Celtic tribe people, to colliers and onwards to the dawn of today, the story of the area's past is detailed within the pages of this very fine book. The authors Maldwyn Griffiths and Richard Herold have carried out their research diligently and I commend their work in the certainty that this history of Gelligaer and its boundaries will be read and re-read many times.

Contents

Introduction

'In tribulation, Gelligaer and my God are my solace'
(Some interesting words from a 10th century poem)

The history of the district that encompasses Gelligaer and its neighbouring villages is a long one, in fact a history that can be traced back almost 2000 years. Some 100 years after Julius Caesar first landed on English shores, the Romans set their sights on Wales and established an early frontier post on the plateaux of Cardiff. Their next move was to explore their way into west and northern Wales and in so doing, one of their routes led onwards to Brecon, necessitating some road construction through Gelligaer; subsequently they built their first garrison camp there in about 75 A.D., a structure of timber and earthen mounds. Numerous excavations have taken place over the years indicating that a more substantial stone-built fort was added somewhere between 103 and 111 A.D. These excavations were soon to be recognised as one of the most important finds of Roman remains in the country. The Romans finally abandoned Britain in about 380 A.D. which led to a period of immigration into Wales, particularly numbers of Irish settlers who brought their Christian teachings and beliefs to Gelligaer.

The next era that was to affect the area was the Norman Period, following William the Conqueror's victory at Hastings in 1066, which led to his establishment as King of England. It was some thirty years thereafter before the Normans made their first appearance at Gelligaer, they meeting with opposition of great ferocity. Despite many reinforcements, they were obliged to beat a hasty retreat in fear of those Welsh natives of Gelligaer, an event that led to the building of Caerphilly Castle in 1268 as a new stronghold to counter any further hindrances from the Rhymney Valley.

All of this important history has already been well-documented and is far beyond the scope of this particular book. This publication deals with the area's history in more modern times, that is to say a *'mere century'*, with the help of more than 200 photographs and as the title suggests, and the photograph on page vi, Gelligaer has spread far and wide since those early years. A number of vitally important structures are included such as St. Catwg's Church of 13th century origin with its ancient parish stocks and Llancaiach Fawr Manor House where King Charles I is said to have stopped for dinner during his campaign for support of the monarchy; these are places of interest to locals and tourists alike.

The dominant industry through the twentieth century was without doubt that of coal, the major employer being Penallta Colliery, the first sod of which was cut in 1905 and led to a plethora of jobs until 1991 when coal-mining came to an end here. There has even been evidence that those ancient Romans made use of this now-redundant mineral during their years of occupation. Wherever there has been a coal-mining industry there has, without exception, been a close and unflappable community spirit and whilst the coal has gone, that community spirit lives on. This is verified when readers start viewing the collection of photographs within these pages. Jazz bands, carnivals and street parties galore from a wide as possible range of years are included, and in many instances will test memories to the hilt. As authors we can hear a few remarks already such as *'what a day that was'*, *'I remember the Silver Jubilee as if it was yesterday'* and *'I just can't remember her first name, that girl sat next to me, but you'd know her I expect, I think she married a Jones and moved away'*.

It is of course these people who *'moved away'* that will enjoy this book as much as anyone, as was the case with our previous publication concerning Ystrad Mynach and Maesycwmmer, with copies finding their way to the most distant parts of the United Kingdom. Finally our grateful thanks are extended to those many good people who allowed us to use their photographic material in this production. Regrettably, due to lack of space some have had to be omitted on this occasion, but then, there is always another day.

1. Gelligaer
2. Penybryn
3. Cascade, Glyn-Gaer & Penpadairheol
4. Penallta Colliery
5. Duffryn
6. Cefn Hengoed
7. Hengoed

CHAPTER 1

Gelligaer

1. William Greenhill and Charles Edwards are quite content to pose for the travelling photographer whilst sitting in the parish stocks in this turn of the century photograph. Edward III decreed the erection of parish stocks in 1376, when it was customary to place culprits of wrong-doing in the stocks as an example to others. In recent years the parish stocks were removed to the church where they are still preserved, note the studs on the bottom of the shoes worn by the two 'wrong-doers'.

2. A delightful view of Castle Hill with the Norman church of St. Cattwgs in the background. It is pleasantly situated at the top of the old road that runs through the village of Gelligaer. The clump of trees on the left of the picture is of historical importance as it surrounds an old hill fort and is known as Twyn y Castell. It is believed to have been the home of Llewelyn Bren, a name of great importance in Welsh History.

3. Horeb Chapel and the chapel cottages with Yew Tree cottages in the background on Castle Hill. Horeb Chapel began its existence in 1848 and is believed to have been built on the site of the old village smithy. Baptisms for the chapel prior to the font being built in, would have been carried out on the Cylla Brook at the bottom of what was the main road through Gelligaer.

4. The Norman church of St. Cattwgs Gelligaer with a clear view of the battlemented clock tower that has become a famous landmark for miles around. In troubled times a fire would be lit on top of the tower to warn neighbouring churches of possible danger of enemy raiders. The Austin and the Ford 8 which are parked outside the Church were probably for a wedding that was taking place inside, with the clock indicating the time being 2.30.

5. Gelligaer Square taken in 1938 and showing Church Houses and the Post Office which was used as the general store for the village. The Postmaster at the time was Tom Brown and his shop assistant was named Iris Williams. She recalls that the Post Office was also known as the local school tuck shop and the children would queue for sweets paying 2 pennies for a quarter of a pound.

6. This painting shows us how the Harp Inn and the square at Gelligaer would have looked like at the turn of the twentieth century. Tommy Spencer did the painting from a sketch drawn by the late Henry Morgan who lived there before the old inn was demolished.

7. The Building of the original hall in Gelligaer in the late 1940s. Jean Williams of the Dyffryn. Mrs. Richards, Mrs. Riley, Olive Jenkins, Mr. And Mrs. Manning, Mr. Jenkins, Frank Rice, Mrs. Elmer, Howard Edwards, George Blewitt, Jack Riley (Treasurer), Towyn Evans are amongst the crowd and were instrumental in the building of the hall.

8. In this photograph Mr. O.B. Greenaway, with a fellow worker and a sturdy pit pony can be seen working at his brother Tom's small drift mine which was located on Gelligaer Mountain.

9. The Harp Inn at Gelligaer stands prominently at the top of the hill adjacent to St. Cattwgs Church and has a unique view of the surrounding countryside. The landlord at the time this photograph was taken was Mr. Rowland Morgan or Rolly, as everyone knew him. Outside the local policeman stands alongside the two females at what was once the main entrance to the public bar. A part of this large building was set aside as the headquarters of the RAOB. Mr. David Edwards and his wife Maureen are the keepers of this fine hostelry at this date of printing of this book.

10. A delightful view of children on the square at Gelligaer taken around 1910. The view shows No.3 Church House with Chapel Cottages and Horeb in the distance. The Post Office to the right of the picture was the main shop for the village. The cost of posting a letter, which would have arrived the next day, was no more than 1/2 penny. Letters from this Post Office would have been sorted at Hengoed sorting office in Raglan Road. Pengam was the nearest telegraph office two miles away. Mrs. Margaret Jones was the sub-postmistress at this time.

11. Harp Terrace which was renamed St. Cattwgs Avenue during the 1960s and is adjacent to the Harp Inn. The prefabs to the right of the picture were home to many of the residents of the village prior to them being knocked down to make way for the new housing estate. Many of the older residents still recall the community spirit of those early days. The little boy has dismounted his tricycle to pose for the photographer on the untarmaced Street.

12. A fine early photograph of the Gelligaer Urban District Council roadlayers. The three men with their shovels and the driver of the steamroller can be seen posing for this photograph outside Gelligaer School.

13. A view of Church Road Cottages Gelligaer which were situated just above St. Cattwgs church, these cottages were demolished for a road-widening scheme in the 1960s. This picturesque scene would rival any other rural scene, with the tower of St. Cattwgs in the distance. The ruins of the Roman fort were near by.

14. William Greenhill as he was known is pictured here in the 1930s at Greenhill farm Church Road Gelligaer, preparing to take a calf to Nelson cattle market. A fine example of the transportation used at this time on the bumpy crude road en route to Nelson. Many older residents of the village will recall a near fateful accident one night during the 1930s, when a bolt of lightning just missed William and killed a cow he was just about to lead into the cow shed.

15. Set in the parish of Gelligaer stands Llancaiach Fawr Manor House which was originally built on a medieval dwelling. The building is a fortified manor house and was the home of Colonel Pritchard. It is noted that Charles I stopped here for dinner while trying to gain support for the Royalist cause. The Manor House has won a Quinquennial Sanford Award for education and is visited by thousands of school-children annually as part of their history studies. Pictured here outside Llancaiach are Esther Griffiths chambermaid, Lady Dalkeith countess and chairperson of the Trust, Suzanne Allen manageress of Llancaiach, Elizabeth Proud seamstress.

16. One of the area's best-known local historians was the late Gethin Thomas who is pictured here with his wife Margaret. He worked as a Coal Board official for the Powell Duffryn Company and then the National Coal Board. He was instrumental in the publication of the book The Gelligaer Story. He was also editor for the Gelligaer Historical Society's publications where he was an active member.

17. Excavation work was carried out on Gelligaer Roman Fort in 1899-1901 by Cardiff Naturalist Society and the cost was said to be around £450. During the summer of 1909 the site adjacent, known as Gaer Fach, was also excavated, the result proving to be of great importance as it consisted of a suite of baths with various furnaces, hot rooms of varying degrees of heat and two plunge baths. Important inscribed stones were discovered, one bearing the name of the Emperor Trojan whilst consul for the fifth time.

18. An excavation carried out in 1963 revealed that the early earth and timber fort to the north-west was of a more permanent camp than first thought. It suggested it was built to accommodate a large garrison of around 1000 infantry or 500 cavalry. It has always been thought that the abandonment of the camp coincided with the building of the stone fort. The view here is of the north-west gate belonging to the stone fort and would have been one of four symmetrically placed on each of the four sides. The Roman camp was reputed to be one of the finest examples of its type in Europe.

19. The Norman church of St. Cattwgs Gelligaer stands on the brow of a hill that has a panoramic view of the countryside. The church would have stood on what was once a wooded highland with the views of neighbouring Bedwellty, Mynyddislwyn and Eglwysilan churches. Although there is no evidence to the building of St. Cattwgs it is thought that its foundations date back to the dark ages and probably built on an old Pagan site. The Normans had a passion for building fine churches and St. Cattwgs is a magnificent example of their work. It is said to have had a peal of bells but these were removed and replaced with a single one, also lost in time are the church's valuables and a priceless very old iron chest that had been removed.

There are references to the church in a Papal Bull issued by Pope Calixtus II in 1119 and again in 1126 by Pope Honorius II, these refer to it as being Cair Castell. Proof of early Celtic faith in the locality is provided by a century Ogam stone, tenth century cross inscribed stone of St. Gwladys and the collection of old poems written around 930 A.D. by a local priest.

The erection of the parish stocks that was decreed by Edward III and once located outside the church are preserved along with the tenth century stone and poems inside the church for safe keeping.

The church today has a dedicated following with a monthly magazine which keeps the parishioners informed on everything going on. The Mothers Union fellowship has regular meetings holding coffee mornings etc. The church has a tower restoration fund with everyone helping to raise money, with organized walks, jumble sales and a 1960s music night in the church hall, all with great success.

20. The inauguration service for Rector Ivor Jones is seen here in this splendid and unique photograph taken by the late D.S. Blatchford in 1949, some of the names are Ivor Jones, Cannon Williams, Arthur Williams (cross bearer), Howard and Keith Derrick, Ron Griffiths, Gethin Lewis, Eddie Bickham, Gwyn Evans, Bobby Lloyd, Gareth Evans, Florrie Price in the front row.

21. Church choir. Back Row: Mrs Rowlands, Mrs. B. John, Mrs. Roberts, Mrs. Cooper, Mrs. O. Jenkins, ?, Mrs. Florrie Price organist, Mrs. Gwillim, Mrs. Nina Morgan, Mrs. Anna Mary Davies, Mrs. Camila Isaac, Ivor Isaac, Gethin Lewis, Ron Wingrove, Rev. Ivor Jones, Emrys Williams, Curate Eaton, Harold Davies, Ken Davies, Harold Derrick, Trevor Carter, Idris Rowlands, Geraint Eynon, Ron Griffiths, Tony Eaton, Mr. Bickham, Gordon Sharp, Keith Derrick, Philip Badham, Howard Derrick, Brian Rowlands, John Cooper, Gareth Evans, Derek Eaton, Arthur Tyrell, Robert Thomas, Gordon Jones, Brian Hall, Gareth Hughes, Graham Fewings, Kenneth Thomas.

22. A wonderful celebration for Mrs. Isaac's 90th birthday at St Cattwgs Church Hall in 1983, it being put on for her by Gelligaer Mothers Union. Mrs. Blanch Nicholas, Mrs. Margaret Partridge, Mrs. Evans, Mrs. Megan Radcliff, Mrs. Gwyneth Price, Mrs. Thomas, Mrs. Pat Davies, Mrs. Margaret Thomas, Mrs. Dilys Prosser, Mrs. Yvonne Martin, Miss Vera Dyer, Miss Gibson, Miss Harry, Miss Frances Woods, Mrs. Joan Jones, Mrs. Pat Davies, Mrs. Margaret Edwards, Mrs. Anne Mary Davies, Rector Clive Jones.

23. Gelligaer Church Passion Play 1935. Yvonne Caple, Dilys Thomas, Gwyneth Williams, Gwyneth Davies, Maybess Morgan, Mrs. Lewis, Mrs. Payne, Brenda Mills, Diana Griffiths, Jane Edwards, Valmai Lewis, Leslie Poulson, Mr. Eynon, Leslie Leigh, Dewi James, Mr. George Callow, Mr. Lewis, Betty Thomas, Gwyn Davies, Hetty Williams, Ginny Edwards, James Lambley, Mary Davies, Ron Biddle, Rachel Payne, George Payne, Mrs Lewis (relay), Violet Eynon.

24. Horeb Chapel stands in a beautiful location on Castle Hill nestled between two old cottages and on the road that once was the main bus route to Bargoed; it is believed it was built on the site of the old village smithy. The founder members were Thomas and Mary Davies. Horeb was once all Welsh speaking and within the walls rich voices soared in four part harmony of magnificent Welsh Hymns. According to the History of the Welsh Baptist denomination, the Hen Dy Cwrdd Chapel, Hengoed was the first Baptist Chapel to be established in the Rhymney Valley. Quite a number of faithful were from Gelligaer. It was decided to establish a place of worship in their own village and Gelligaer became a branch of Hengoed Chapel in 1842-1845. For the first year it was known as Gelligaer and afterwards Y Pente and was established in 1846. Nothing more was heard of the cause until 1848 when Gelligaer was accepted into the Cymanfa of Welsh Baptists at Hirwaun. Morgan Jones who became Minister of Education in a Labour Government was brought up as a boy and teenager at Horeb and pronounced publicly that he was proud of the fact that he received his basic fundamental Christian training at the chapel, which helped him to mould his life and career. There are many others who believe this to be true, two brothers Rev. Thomas Richards Brecon and Rev. Glyndwr Richards of Caerphilly, were both splendid bilingual preachers of repute, both products of Y Capel Bach ar y bryn, translated as 'the little chapel on the hill'. Major W. Williams M.B.E.L, L.R.A.M and former bandmaster of the Gordon Highlanders and Metropolitan Police Band. Mr. Alan Richards F.T.S.C. of Pencerdd Glasfryn, a composer of note, voice trainer, music teacher and conductor. His son Brynley was Deacon and organist for 50 years. The first wedding at the chapel was Morwen Richards and David Price who created front-page news in the Rhymney Valley Express. Although the membership is somewhat depleted there is still the faithful few who hope for a revival in Christian beliefs. Emlyn Richards who is the oldest member and trustee of the chapel was once correspondent for the Rhymney Valley and Merthyr Express newspaper, he is proud of his family involvement and commitment to the chapel.

25. The cast of this Nativity play at Horeb Chapel in 1960 is Mr. Ron Harding, Morwen Price, Mary Bray, Gareth Bray, ? Baines, Keith Harding, Julie Marsden, Jackie Marsden, Susan Bray, David Price, Judith Evans, Ann Jenkins, Kath, Susan Jenkins, Nickolas Popodic. Possible Andrew Jenkins?

26. When the Whitsun parade came around each year it was quite a treat for all the children, for some it was the only time during the year that new clothes would be bought for them. They always loved marching around the streets and the tea party and the games that followed. This photograph shows the Whitsun walkout on Castle Hill with Mr Brynley Richards conducting the singing with the following people in the parade - Tom Davies, Emlyn Richards, Mrs. Blatchford and Mrs. Ceinwen Roberts who are the teachers of the primary school section of the Welsh Chapel. Gillian Arthur, Janice James, Jean McCutcheon, Gwyneth Richards, Christopher Jenkins, Elfed Beddoe, Glyn Bassett, The Blackman brothers and David Davies.

27. A Whitsun walkout of Horeb Chapel as it makes it way up past White City and on to Gelligaer. Mrs. Blatchford who was very prominent in the chapel is seen here leading the singing during one of the stops. Mrs. Blatchford accompanied by Morwen Richards, Jean McCutcheon, Gwyneth Richards, Blanch Richards, Wendy Bray, Tony Morgan.

28. A well organized photograph taken on Castle Hill showing members of Horeb Chapel during 1948. Some of the names are Mrs. Blatchford, Emlyn Richards, Lionel Hughes, Morwen Richards, Gwyneth, Jean Davies, John Bray, Blackman Brothers, Ray, Tony Morgan, Alan Walker, Sid Thomas, Joan James, Caenwen Roberts, Mr. Gideon Roberts, Brynley Richards, Edgar Jenkins-Royal stores Glyngaer, Elwyn Wathen, Rita Williams, Jean Phillips, Mary Bray, Alwyn Evans, Clive Phillips, Christopher Jenkins, John Davies, Mary Hughes, George David, Audrey Christian, Miss Eunice Price, Elred Beddoe, Monica Ward, Mair Hughes.

29. The church hall has been used for meetings, presentations, plays and also a Sunday School, On this occasion it was put to use by the church operatic in the 1950s play *The Magic Key*. Included in the cast were Shirley Derrick, Brian Rowlands, Royston Marlow, Myra Price, Florence Jones, Jean Marlow, Dawn Carter, ?, Clive Evans, Phyllis Horrell, Clive Howard, Brenda Sinett, ? Jones, Howard Derrick, Keith Derrick, Bernice Fewings, Georgina Snare, Val Oliver.

30. The Gelligaer Peace March seen in this photograph shows the marchers passing the Dyffryn Cottages on the old road to Gelligaer that passed through Glyn-Gaer. The Plough & Harrow public house can be seen in the distance and just below this were a few cottages named Tai Charles that have since been demolished. It was one of many Peace Marches that took place throughout Britain in 1919 to celebrate the end of the First World War, which finally came to an end in November 1918.

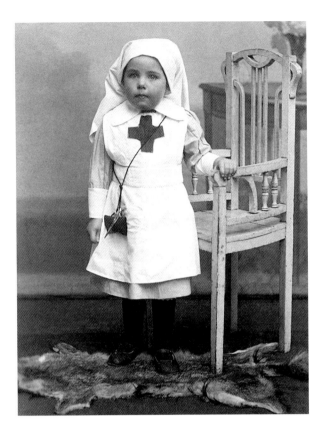

31. The little nurse in this 1919 photograph is Iris May Williams or Iris Greenhill as she was known. Dressed in the Red Cross outfit that was manufactured using authentic Red Cross material. Her outfit won her first prize in the Peace March and Carnival at Gelligaer (shown on page 24). And as a little girl she remembered the day being very hot and being carried up Castle Hill where people were making a fuss of her and recalls walking past the judges of the fancy dress competition where she won the £3 first prize. The Red Cross outfit was used by the society for fund raising and from her home in Gelligaer she is still raising money to this day.

32. Gelligaer red cross with Alice Thomas, Mrs. Elsie Ward, Mrs. Arscott, Vera Dyer, Lorna Hann, Mrs. Douglas Hann, Gwyneth Thomas and Mrs. Dyer amongst the dedicated supporters.

33. Gelligaer Girls Jazz Band. Wendy Lewis, Gail Leeman, Sandra Barnes, Siân O'Hagan, Gloria Garbutt, Tina Burke, Wendy Wallington, ?, Lucille Carter, Viv Cook, Sharon Gilbert, Susan Powell, Sharon Thomas, Lynette Moon, Carol Ansell, Mandy Lewis, Jackie Atkinson, Elaine Angel, Julie Forrest, Jane Marlow, Pat Taylor, ?, Lyn Rees, Carol Davies, Sheryl Davies, Eileen Hopkins, Sheryl Williams, Gerald Haydn who later joined the Welsh Guards.

34. A line up for this mid 1960s photograph of the Stewardesses jazz band, include Susan Morgan, ?, Lyn Beech, Mandy Lewis, ?, Vivian Cook, Caroline Murphy, Rita Ackerman, Wendy Lewis, Mandy Moon, Janet Davies, Maria Derrick, Pat Taylor, Carol Davies, Lesley Gorham, Sandra Kent, Ann Edwards, Audrey Davies, Karen Jones, ?, Debbie Moore, Sandra Haydn, Sheryl Willits, Paulene Haydn, Julie Roberts. In the front Donald Willts, Bill Willets, Gerald Haydn, Steve Jones.

35. The Gelligaer Stewardesses Jazz Band, World Junior Jazz Band winners in the 1970s proudly display their trophy. The photograph was taken with the backdrop of a magnificent set of other trophies won by the band. Special thanks are given to Fred and Doris Reynolds who dedicated their lives to the village jazz band and helping to bring the World Cup to the area. In the photograph are Anthony Thomas, Jane Marlow, Brent Mackintosh, Maria Price, Deborah Williams, Gillian Court, Cheryl Davies, Julie Court, Cheryl Crump, Tina Porter, Wendy Edwards, Julie Wallington, Phillip Lewis, Nigel Murphy, Alison Marlow, Diane Edwards, Alison Jones, Sarah Davies, Suzanne Price, Sandra Morgan, Maureen Pritchard, Gaynor Morgan, Alison Morgan, Helen Marlow.

21

36. The Boxing Club was started in the Harp Hotel Gelligaer during the late 1960s by founder member Charles Hill or 'Charlo' as everyone knew him. The first trainer at the club was Kenny Harrison and he quickly got it recognized as a boxing club. They moved to Penybryn hall for a short time before moving to their present premises in Gelligaer. Some names to be noted are the first chairman Terry Cornice followed by Kenny Harrison, Gerry Carney and Geoff Price a committee member who was always at the heart of everything, from helper to Father Christmas at parties. Some of the early members of the boxing club display their trophies and medals during the 1960s namely Sid Carter, Ray Owens, Alan Haydn, Sandra Wilding, Ken Williams, Eamon Doonan, Terry Denham, Anthony Harrison.

37. Over the years the boxing club has taken many a youngster off the streets and shown them self discipline, and in turn, the lads have helped turn the club into the most successful in the Rhymney Valley. These young boxers proudly extend their chests for this photograph which includes Des Thomas, John Lemin, Brian Reynolds, Fred Rice, Wyndam Evans, Granville Davies, ?, ?, Phil Rogers, Gerwyn Davies, Robert Quirk, Peter Powell, Lyn Horsman.

38. Three Welsh Champions show an excellent example of the standard of talent at Gelligaer Amateur Boxing Club, as they proudly display their Welsh vests. The club is noted for its ability in producing some of the finest Welsh and British schoolboy champions in Wales. Standing in between Billy Summers and Kenny Harrison are, Jonathan Lloyd, Daniel Phelps 'Boone' and Craig Sullivan. Dai Gardiner trainer and manager and Gary Thomas and Pat Chidgey who use the club on professional nights have produced some outstanding World and European WBO and IBF champions with the likes of Steve Robinson and Robbie Reagan to name two.

39. Some of the members of Gelligaer boxing club are pictured here at the club, including Steve Thomas, Darren Reeks, Dylan Bull, Dan Underwood, Keyron O'Sullivan, Craig O'Sullivan, Woody Greenaway, Paul Cook, ? Liam, Gareth Owens, Nathan O'Sullivan, Chris Pope, Keith Jones, Daniel 'Boone' Phelps, Jonathan Lloyd. The trainers were Jason Summers, Paul Greenaway, Darren Underwood with the club being sponsored by Alfred Hawker.

40. These party revellers can't wait to get the photography session completed and get tucked into the fine spread laid out in this street party held in Heol Penallta. The revellers include John Edwards, Maureen Edwards, Pat Swan, Miss Richards, Maureen Whitcombe, Ann Davies, Christine Davies, Mr. & Mrs. Harding, Jackie Davies, Tommy Davies, Kenny Davies, Mrs. Smith, David Smith, Paul Smith, Brenda Sinett, Mrs. Honeywill, Tony Honeywill, Sheila Honeywill, Noreen Vaughan, Carol or Elaine Vaughan.

41. This photograph is of a Maypole and the Maypole dancers on one of the carnival floats in the 1950s from the prefabs in Gelligaer. The residents of Heol Y Waun were part of a close knit community. The float is making its way to the carnival field; the only names found were that of Grace and Winnie King.

42. Gelligaer Party and another chance to recall those prefab days in the 1950s this time with the top end of Heol y Waun, some of the people are Alwen Evans, Shirley Davies, Pamela Evans, Tom Evans, Betty Boulton, Alan Boulton, Jeff Jones, Dai Gardiner, Johnny ?, David Jenkins, George ?.

43. Residents of Heol y Waun prefabs lower end are all prepared for their street party in this 1953 photograph of the Coronation celebrations with Reverend Jones about to say grace. Some names traced include Mrs. Bond, Mrs. Lil Harding, Dot Shemwell, Mrs. Amor, Rev. Jones, Julie Shemwell, Grace King, Jessie Harding, Joan Gardner, Winnie King.

44. When your street happens to be the main road, the obvious place to hold a party is in the field opposite. These residents of Church Road did just that in 1969, the year of the Prince of Wales Investiture, in the Roman Field as shown in this photograph. To be seen are David Williams, Graham Downs, Pat Smith, Gloria Garbutt, V. Garbutt, Miriam Greening, Raymond Norman, Donna Smith, Olive Queen Evans, ? John.

45. The Edward Lewis charity school was established in 1760 and was close to Gelligaer Church and adjacent to the Roman fort. Edward Lewis died in 1728 and he made provisions in his will for the building of a school for fifteen poor boys of the parish and the salary of a schoolmaster, the first schoolmaster being Reverend George Parry who was curate at Gelligaer. The building resembled a cottage comprised of a large room on the ground floor that was later divided into two, the upper floor being the living quarters for the schoolmaster. The school was demolished in 1964 in what was so-called progress of road widening and at the time, unfortunately was not classed as a listed building.

46. Pictured here are some of the residents of Dan Y Gaer Rd Gelligaer in 1977. It was one of the many street parties that were held in the village to celebrate the Queen's Jubilee. After all the hard work of preparation it was time for some of the residents to sit back and enjoy the afternoon such as Cliff Buffton, Martha Buffton, Maureen Edwards, Vicky Edwards, Mavis Rees, Margaret Pearce, Margaret Lundigan.

47. A happy crowd of youngsters of Dan Y Gaer Rd Gelligaer are about to sit down for one of the Street parties that were held to mark the Silver Jubilee in 1977. To be seen are Wendy Edwards, Susan Rees, Christopher Rees, Julie Roberts Lesley Roberts, Sian Thomas Virginia Lane, ? Lewis, Chris Horton.

48. A visit to Guinness Brewery at Park Royal London with Fred Evans and a party of local constituents on November the 24th 1972, a photograph obviously taken before they tasted the brewery samples. When Don, landlord of the Cross Inn said it was impossible to arrange a visit to the brewery, Fred Evans M.P. was quickly on the phone to the office and within two months a visit was arranged. Some of the visitors recall they all went into the Toucan bar where everything was free and were quick to sample a Guinness or two. Some of the names are (Top) Cyril Flook, Stan Drayton, Duncan Powell Mr. Crocker, Mal Evans, Idris George, (Middle) Billy Chandler, Thomas Evans, Melvyn Evans, Ted. (Bottom) Don Shortman landlord of the Cross Inn, Dennis Murphy, Fred Evans M.P., Ricky Vaughan, Rowland Hughes, Maurice Evans.

49. Ever since the first bus service ran between Bargoed and Ystrad Mynach via Gelligaer in 1928, wintry conditions have played role in making this part of the route sometimes a little tricky. In this photograph the bus was at the top of Pengam Road on Gelligaer Hill when a car coming down the hill skidded on an icy patch on the road and hit the bus sideways. The bus in turn started a slide that eventually sent it over the banking; fortunately there were no injuries in this incident.

50. A well organised and composed photograph of the children of Harp Terrace around the 1930s. Though it might look more of a school photograph, the photographer had brought these children together while playing out in the street. Some of the children are from the families of the Mitchells, Mathews, Govier, Howells, Pritchard and Williams.

51. With this 1961 view of Harp Terrace in the background, this Gelligaer family, Mrs. Elaine Harris nee Morgan with her children Linda, Glenys and Patricia pose proudly for the photographer.

52. County Councillor Keith Derrick pictured in the centre of the picture during his term of office in 1999-2000. An active member for the area and list of credits to his name are 1984 becoming Community Councillor; vice chairman in 1988 and two years as chairman in 1989 and 99. In 1994 he became Mid Glamorgan County Councillor. He organised a campaign for the lights and crossing in Penpedairheol, and with Granville Davies and Bob Summers they were founder members of the Cascade and Penpedairheol allotment society. Gelligaer Youth Club was another success along with Brian Martin and Sheila Davies. The Cascade, Penpedairheol and Glyngaer reunions were started in 1999 with lifelong friend Billy Chandler and are very popular with people coming from as far away as London, Shrewsbury and Hereford etc. He is also noted for being the last councillor to be elected for the Mid Glam Cascade Ward before the change over to the County Borough. Back Row: Councillors Judith Pritchard, Tom Mathews, Hevin Wynn David, David Smith, Robert Thomas, Mary Richards. Front Row: Allan Angel, June Cook vice chairman, Keith Derrick chairman, Ann Davies clerk, Dennis Bolter.

53. The Gelligaer Midshipmen are pictured here marching through the village of Coleford in Gloucestershire in 1960. The Midshipmen Jazz Band, who, like their predecessors the Stewards set high professional standards and their ability of winning jazz band championships wherever competing. Their much admired uniforms were some of the best ever seen in the country and always won rounds of applause from everyone. Some of the names are Gilbert Davies bandleader; John Tucker, Leyshon Davies, Ron Davies, Donald Rees, Cyril Tucker, Henry Lewis, Bill Willits the instructor; the little boy is David 'Taffy' Williams, and Mr. Horrell with the pipe.

54. A photograph of Miss Mandy Moon beauty queen, Lyn ?, Michelle Vining, Beaty Moses, William Coombs, Mr. Coombs, Carol Morley, Olwen Noaks, Dilys Jones, Julie, Fred Reynolds, Sandra Haydn, Beauty Queen Miss Mandy Moon and member of Ystrad Mynach Jazz Band the Majorettes is pictured here in this late 1960s carnival at Gelligaer. Mr. Fred Reynolds who is seen here on the left of the picture was much a part of celebrations of the day, as he was instrumental in the standard of professional qualities needed to win many of the jazz band championships.

55. Lisa Watts, Adele Arthur, Shelly Osborne, Alma Jones, Jane Forrest, Yvonne Lewis, Gail Maiden, Vicky Edwards, Lisa Bannister, Tracy Woods, Ceri Wallington, Siân Porter, Kelly Davies. A group of the Gelligaer Stewardesses Jazz Band have plenty to celebrate after another successful competition during the 1980s.

56. A very jubilant crowd of young lads is more than happy to pose for this 1980s photograph after winning the Rhymney Valley Sunday League. The Harp Inn football team celebrating in fine style as they display their trophies, and its drinks all round. The team consisted of Mark Lewis, Graham Crocker, John Thomas, Adrian Phelps, Tony Edwards, Craig Davies, Brian Corns, Phillip Andrews, Ozzy, Dean Davies, Robert Andrews, Carl Andrews, Mark Andrews.

57. The Harp Inn Darts Team. who were some of the Rhymney Valley's top players in the 1950s. They are - back: Ken Franklyn, Mexy Moore, Billy Thomas, Sid Carter, Gordon Bishop. Front: Tommy Murphy, Nally Pritchard, Manny Powell, Mel James (Landlord), Dennis Martin.

58. Gelligaer Jusin-Do Karate Club 2002. Wyndam Boobier (class instructor 3rd Dan), Louise Gilbert, Sarah Davies, Gemma Matuszczyk, Jennifer Clerk, Tony Salmon, Geraint Whitcombe, Laura Hayes, Samantha Whitcombe, Emma Hopkins, Paul Davies, Jessica Sayer, Scott Hennessy, James Stone, Stephanie Stone, Martyn Evans, Liam Williams, Luke Hilton, Lewis Hayes, Joshua Thomas, David Gregory, Shaun Gregory, Alex Davies, Amberley Crimmings.

CHAPTER 2

Penybryn

59. Penallta Colliery the construction of which began in 1905 was a provider of jobs in the district for eighty years with a 3,208 manpower at its peak in the 1930s and producing around 860,000 tons, output per year. The Powell Duffryn Steam Coal Company, one of the largest such companies, owned the colliery and who at their peak in the 1930s owned some 75 collieries. The picture shown above is of No.2 upcast shaft during the 1940s.

60. A general view of Penallta Colliery taken from the Graig Hengoed. In the distance may be seen Penybryn Terrace, known as the forty houses, these being the first to be built in Penybryn. Numbers 1 and 2 shafts stand prominently in the centre of the picture with the conveyor belt leading to the washery and there are hundrds of Powell Duffryn trucks waiting to be loaded on the Cylla branch of GWR's extension from Ystrad Mynach.

61. A fine photograph of the colossal cooling towers with a bellow of steam coming from the exhaust; the ponds around the cooling towers were a popular place for the youngsters to have a swim in the summer months.

62. This interior photograph shows the colliery powerhouse with the winder for the downcast shaft in the distance and is a fine example of the high quality engineering that was necessary to run this type of industry efficiently.

63. A scene long gone, the buckets full of the waste slag with the safety nets underneath ready to catch any loose waste. The buckets would travel towards the huge slagheaps that used to dominate the skylines. The twin shafts stand prominently in the distance, as do the towers.

64. A 1940 photograph of the huge Penallta washery building dominating the skyline while basking in the sunlight with Hengoed and Cefn Hengoed visible in the distance, while all the empty coal trucks await their load.

65. This group of miners posing for the photographer shows the enormity of the winding wheels that were used at the Penallta colliery.

66. On a visit to Penallta Colliery by Mostyn Richard who is shown to the right of Colliery Maintenance Engineer Timmy Evans, he had an experience he will never forget. During the tour he walked a few miles underground where he started a Panza Machine and cut a piece of coal for a keepsake that he will treasure with this memory.

67. Graham Munkley and fellow miners huddle in the pit cage waiting for the descent that will take them 2000ft to the bottom of the shaft and then a possible walk of two miles or more to his work area.

68. The Rhymney Valley womens' support group is pictured here leading the men back to work at Penallta after a long hard struggle to save the mine from closure. Some of the support group recall themselves marching with the miners in London, on the picket line continually and in the soup kitchens with people being very generous and sympathetic to the struggle. They are pictured here marching through Gelligaer at 5am ready for the morning shift and some of the names are Judith Pritchard, Carol Evans, Betty Elliot, Pam, Sonja, Graham Hughes, David McCarthy, and Ray Price.

69. Some of the canteen staff at Penallta Colliery are pictured here during the early 1960s. They would have been a welcoming sight to the men after working a shift at the mine and provide them with that much needed refreshing cup of tea. There are plans by Caerphilly County Borough Groundwork to develop the disused canteen into a visitor centre. With only a few names of staff given they are Ann Davies, Berth Caswell, Muriel Heaven, Mrs. Thomas.

70. Penallta Canteen staff 1940s-50s. Lil Porter, Heather Partridge, Bertha Plummer the cook.

71./72. Pictured are two of the early football teams from the village and were called for some unknown reason the Penybryn Pals. The army reserve poster can clearly be seen behind the top photograph taken in 1917 and only one name is known and that is of Mr. Bill Owen. The bottom photograph taken in the late 1920s includes Bill Owen, Mr. Lewis, Jim Turner, Bob Cadwallader. ? Williams. The team also had someone with a profession of a rat catcher. Although a little camera shy the team's mascot can be seen on the lap of one of the front players.

73. Penallta NCB cup finalists 1957. Ted Cook, John Digby, Peter Blewitt, Ponty Jones, Graham Moore, Clive Jones, Dai Brooks, Jacky Griffiths, Bill Mills, Derek Lewis, Michael Palmer, Gareth Owen, Clive Bruton, Ray Price, Billy Flew.

74. A Penallta NCB Cricket team and some followers in the 1950s. Taken in the grounds of Ystrad Fawr NCB offices. They include Ted Cook, John the bobby, Clive Jones, Mr. Bill Flew, Ponty Jones, Ray Beddoe, ? Saunders.

75. Most of the lads shown in this photograph are from Penybryn and were active members of Ystrad Mynach Boys Club back in the 1960s. Taken on a week away at St. Athans Boys Village are Peter Reynolds, Glen Carlow, Glyn Davies, Brian Clifford, Dave Thomas. Middle row: Andrew Morris, Philip Price, Gareth James, Chris Sharp (Club Leader), John Davies, Glen Rees. Bottom: Robert Evans, Steve Jones.

76. Penybryn has over the years produced some fine sportsmen and successful football teams. Shown here is the Penybryn A.F.C. team who won the Rhymney Valley Senior Cup Final, that was played at Brithdir Park 1984. Back Row. D. Lewis, Brian Reynolds, P. Andrews, Colin Morgan, Paul Rowlands, Mal Court, W. Pritchard, A. Davies. Front. K. Breeze, Billy Gorden, Nigel Price, Graham 'Curly' Morgan, Colin Kirkham.

77. A photograph of the Penybryn under 16 football team, which was taken before their game played in Treowen. Back Row: I. Martin, J. Ward, B. Reynolds, T. Price, Front. T. Barry, B. Arthur, R. Milsom, T. McCarthy, G. Lockyer, A. Lewis, J. Smith. Sitting on fence B. Bier, G. Rees.

78. This photograph shows Penybryn A.F.C. prior to their game played in Quakers Yard 1950, many of the children belonging to these players followed in their footsteps and turned out for their local team in the years to follow. Back: L. Rees (Trainer), B. Broad, N. Price, Snowy Price, T. Murphy, G. Davies. Front. E. James, F. Boobier, S. Reynolds, G. Franklyn, D. Silcox, K. Franklyn.

79. Behind the bar is the Steward and Stewardess Melvin and Cassie Bowers, with the help of Albert and Shirley Edmunds who never let them down on busy nights. Melvin and Cassie were at the opening of the club during the 1960s and remember the Welsh rugby team playing a strong Penallta side and them attending a buffet in the night. A signed ball and team photograph from the visiting Welsh team became a prize memento.

80. Penallta Rugby Club always had a good following and their supporters were willing to travel far and wide to follow their team. Here we see a crowd of happy lads on their way to the north of England on their Middlesborough tour. Dai Edwards of the Harp Inn Gelligaer was the team coach and he recalls that he had a tap on the Harp door at 6 o'clock in the morning by the keen touring team but after an early morning drink they didn't get away until midday, some six hours behind schedule. Some of the lads seen here in fine spirits include Lee Ackerman, Jeff Davies, Dai Jones, Paul Rogers, Gary Morgan, Alan Osborne, Smiler, Tichy Davies, Rufus Thomas, Tyron Bullock, Dunky, Dai Flanagan, Wayne Jones and Phil.

81. Always one of the highlights of the season is the club's presentation night and dinner and here we see some of the team who received an award for their endeavour throughout the season. Back Row: Nigel James, Sam Smith, Paul Ferris, Dean Hanson, Mike Williams, Phil Morris, Eddie Rogers. Middle. Bob Griffin, Dean Woods, Brian Corns, Mike Guilfoyle, Mike Thomas. Front. Wayne Davies, Des Rees, Neil Roberts, Tyron Bullock, Paul Hollifield.

82. A reunion of past players of Penallta rugby club took place on their 50th anniversary on 5th April 2002. It gave the club's photographer Dino Spenetti a chance to catch this unique picture opportunity of past captains. Included in the photograph is former British Lion Dai Watkins who played outside half for Wales during the 1960s. Also pictured are Steve Tucker, Mervin Payne, Leighton John, Darren Hooper, Johnny Morgan, Dai Flanagan, Huw Stephens, Des Rees, Jason Griffiths, Lee Ackerman, Dai Watkins, Lance Phillips, Craig Phillips, Mike Thomas, Bob Fowler, Cyril Payne, Ponty Jones, Clive Jones, ? Morgan, Brian Cornes and Steve Richards.

83. A fine early photograph of the Penybryn Junior Jazz Band 1946-47. Standing. C. Horrell, T. Jones, Mr. Wood, G. Edwards, K. Price, Mr. Atkinson, R. Dainton, A. Whitefoot, G. Jones, G. Wood, T. Morgan, K. Spiller, D. Lewis, T. Watkins, Mr. Reynolds, M. Jones, M. Heaven, C. Reynolds. Kneeling. C. Brick, S. Thomas, Pritchard, D. Williams, C. Lewis, Atkinson, A. Reynolds, D. Rees, Atkinson, H. Link, R. King, R. Lewis, W. Lewis, R. Davies, T. Arthur, J. Wood, C. Davies, R. Davies.

84. The ladies of Penybryn are letting their hair down in this 1969 photograph of the carnival group in fancy dress. Included in this group are, Anita Morris, Marg Heydon, Joyce James, Jenny Spiller, Ann Tucker, Lou Beer, Margaret Padfield, Joyce Smyth, Peggy Smyth, Doreen Jenkins, Shirley Lewis,Olive Murphy, Lil Porter, Pam Jones, Dilys Jones, Jill Paget, Linda Collins, Dorris Reynolds, Dulcia Woods, Muriel Arthur.

85. A proud moment for John Wood from Penybryn when he met the Prince of Wales during a visit to the old site of Penallta Colliery in the late 1990s. John, who was chairman of the finance council at Ystrad Fawr had worked at Penallta for 40 years with the last 15 of those as a ventilation officer. Also in the picture are Maldwyn Davies Chief Executive and Pat Mears planning officer of the County Borough Council.

86. Welsh handball champion 1927-35 Ken Lockyear pictured here with his wife Margaret at their home in Penybryn. In 1927 he challenged and beat the master player Bert Morgan. Ken was noted for his speed and earned the title Flashy, Ken was also one of the Famous 25 who went on strike by staging a 60 hour sit-in at Penallta in 1948 for colliers not receiving full pay.

87. One of the finest examples of a well-organized jazz band and family tradition of following in their father's footsteps are the Wood family from Penybryn. The Jazz Band was called the Stewards and later went on to change their name to the Gelligaer Midshipmen. Pictured here in the 1940s are Jack Wood bandleader, Donald Wood front ranker and Gerald Wood the mascot.

88. A fine view looking over to Penallta Colliery from the Graig Hengoed. Penybryn can be seen just beyond Penallta and this village was built to house the mineworkers and their families, whereby the fine houses of Penallta Villas and Duffryn Street in the foreground were built for the colliery managers and officials. Penalltau Isaf Farm viewed on the left was the home of Thomas Llewelyn born in 1720 he was mostly remembered for his campaign to publish more Welsh Bibles and by 1769 more than 20,000 had been published.

89. At the time this photograph was taken this mode of transport was quite a luxury. Will the Rocks as he was known, is proud to show off his new motorbike and sidecar with Mrs. Howells as his lady passenger. Penalltau Isaf Farm was the setting and the Penallta Villas provide the backdrops for this photograph.

90. Seen here is a superb 1947-1948 photograph of the Penybryn Page Boys Jazz Band taken outside the Fox and Hounds public house. R. Davies, D. Osborne, G. Woods, S. Thomas, K. Spiller, G. Puddifoot, G. Robinson, D. Williams, F. Davies, C. Brick, D. Lewis, T. Jenkins, B. Steed, C. Spillar, C. Lewis, R. Owen, G. Edwards, K. Rice, S. Davies, T. Morgan, J. Jenkins, D. Owen, A. Whitefoot, A. Walker, G. Tucker, T. Watkins, C. Horrel, C. Reynolds.

91. Penybryn St. John Ambulance 1950s. Howell George, Graham Munkley, John Wood, Norman Rogers, Clive Phillips, Bert Hopley, Tommy Pritchard, Dai Thomas the farm. Charlo Hill, Phill Dare, ? Rogers, Fred Caswell, Des Dolaway, Dilwyn Reynolds, Joe Doonan, George Woods, ? Caswell, Lionel Hughes, Bernard Arthur, Alan Harigan, ? Rees, Alan Evans.

92. A grand crowd of Penybryn pensioners posing on the steps of their hotel The Cavendish Court Hotel Blackpool. Amongst them are Mrs. Olive James, Mrs. Rebecca Quirk, Mrs. Peggy Scudamore, Mrs. Silcox, Mrs. Caswell, Mr. James, Doris Winters, Mrs. James, Mrs. Harding, Mrs. Arthur, Maggie Jones, Peggy Smyth.

93. A pleasant group posing in front of their coach whilst on their stay at Blackpool in the early 1960s, and included in the group are Betty Boulten, Brenda Boobier, Freddy Boobier, Derek Lewis, Brenda Lewis, Mr. Parker, Mrs. Parker.

94. A sunny day for this Penybryn family coach outing to Barry and included in the group are Bobby Fowler, Cliff Reynolds, Besse Brooks, Mrs. Hole, Alf Tucker, Alwyn Reynolds, Alice Thomas, Ann James, Joan Reynolds, Ceinwen Evans, Terry Quirk, Percy Reynolds, Brian Reynolds, Mervyn Jones, Dorothy Brooks, Susan Brooks, Dianne Brooks, David Evans.

95. Penybryn Street Party in 1969. Back: Winnie Darch, Margaret Hill, Audrey Barnett, Elizabeth Jenkins, Mrs Mullins, Dolly Thomas, Mrs.Griffiths, Joyce Jenkins, Linda Caswell. Front: Dora Franklin, Gwladys Batt, ?, Val Pritchard, Irene Caswell

96. These youngsters of Penybryn stand together for this 1949 photograph. T. Pritchard, B. Andrews, R. Woods, H. Owen, T. Price, C. Owen, B. Brick, D. Price, O. Smirten, E. Jones, M. Jones, T. Quirk, B. Reynolds, R. Quirk, T. Tucker, J. Reynolds, E. Jones, N. Reynolds, H. Price, S. Reynolds.

97. Before the opening of Calvary Penybryn people used to walk to Bethel in Cefn Hengoed and sometimes required the aid of lighted candles in jam jars during the dark evenings. It was decided to hold meetings at the home of Mr. Greening and with the formation of a committee and trustees, work began on the building of Calvary in 1927 with much of the work being done voluntarily. Calvary was opened in April 1928 and a combined Whit-Monday march between Bethel and Calvary Sunday schools took place. Fun and games and a tea party followed the march. The Whitsun tea party and walkout was always a favourite and everyone looked forward to having something new to wear. Pictured here during the 1950s in Penybryn having fun and games are: Rolly Edmunds, Janice Hughes, Diane Skidmore, Lillian Skidmore, Jean Pritchard, Gillian Arthur, John Wakley, Desmond Parry, Beverly Parry, Andrew ?, Steven Edmunds, Denise Lewis.

98. The Penallta tradesmen are seen here enjoying their Christmas get together at the Tylers Arms Nelson. Ken Davies, Ozzy, Brian Adams, Albert Carey, Noel Jones, Terry Frowen, Terry Ash, Gordon Puddyfoot, Ken Franklin, Donald Silcox, John Amos, Jerry Lewis, Ronald Hancox, Clive Phillips, Johnny Davies, Clive Pearce, Alvin Royal.

99. St. John Ambulance 1960s Church Hall Gelligaer. Joe Doonan, Frederick Caswell, Dilwyn Reynolds, ?, Billy Paget, Ron Michel, Greg Lucas, Phil Dare, Janet Court, Jean Caswell, Margaret Jones, Janice James, Mrs. Hickey, Sandra Plummer, ?, Jeffery Wood, ?, -?, Eirion Gatfield, ?, ?, John Cobley, Mr. Munkley, Bert Hopley. The photo on the back wall is of Olive Jenkins.

100. This delivery of coal having been unloaded on to the street in was once a common sight throughout Britain, when coal was the main fuel source available. We can see that as children Colin Wailey, Marilyn Jones and Peter Reynolds have found the dirtiest location to pose for the photographer in this 1955 photograph.

101. Penybryn Coronation Fancy Dress. In this fancy dress Cowboy and Indians the only names to date are R. Quirk, T. Quirk and Mrs. Rebecca Quirk.

102. A happy bunch patiently posing for this photograph including Billy Underwood, Dennis Jones, Wyndham Lewis, Theo Jenkins, Shirley Martin, Joan Chiddy, G. Woods, Graham Fewings, Thelma Rees, Derek Lewis, John Griffiths, Susan Powell, Percy Court.

103. Penybryn party by the swings on the playground. Mrs. Paterson, Mrs. Thomas, Mrs. Griffiths, Mrs. Jenkins, Gwyneth Morgan, Dolly Thomas, Mrs. Rees, Olive Jones, Mrs. Jones, Mr. Rees, Margaret Rees.

104. Pictured outside the Fox and Hounds is this float of Penallta Colliery and was the Penybryn entry in a Cascade carnival during the 1990s. The float was decorated around the sides showing various stages of mining. This finely decorated entry won tremendous applause from all who saw it. Some of the miners are David Exton, Rhiann Rogers, Amy Crocker, Siobhan Thomas, Michael Britain, Laura Cox.

105. This photograph was taken at the Taff Trailers in Quakers Yard and this group of ladies, having something to celebrate are enjoying their evening. The ladies skittle team from the Fox and Hounds in Penybryn became the highest scoring team in the Nelson League in 2000. The ladies in a fun mood are Geraldine Morgan, Liz Jones, Karen Magyar, Mandy Williams, Karen Edwards, Marilyn Boucher, Angela Parker, Glenys Parker, Fay Murphy, Jenny ?.

106. VJ celebrations 1995 in Trosnant Crescent was a street party to remember and included are some names. Glenys and David Parker, Angela Parker, Gareth Parker, Alison, Jeffrey and Rhiannon Greenaway, Paul and Julie Rogers, Wayne Morgan, Lyndsey Thomas, Samantha Jane Boobier, Linda Boobier, Samantha Wheeler, Billy Jones, Carol Morley, Mandy Morley, Mrs. Harris, Kathryn, David, Louise and Victoria Baker, Wyndam and Doreen Thomas, Liz Davies, Mary Clifford, Doris Winters, Marie Wheeler, Dean Wheeler, Anthony Lewis Tracy Lewis, Corey Lewis, Dwayne Greenway, Carmen Evans, Rhiann Rogers, Lisa Evans, Brent Fox, Christopher ?, Kelly Anthony, Michael Anthony, Gloria Anthony, Vera Hall, Miss Vera Dyer, Joyce Evans, Doreen Jenkins Margaret Hill, Mrs. Barnard, Carol ?

107. The Trosnant Hillbillies float was a tremendous success in the 1970s and brought a lot of fun to the Penybryn carnival. With Jed Clampet and family are Ron Wheeler, Susan Jones, Helen Maloney, Betty Woods, Joan Reeves, Louise Reeves, Angela Griffiths, Lynn Jones, Eileen Shirley, Leanne Shirley and not forgetting whiskey-drinking Grandma Clampet who was Joyce James.

108. When you think of Hawaii you automatically think of sunshine but not on this day for this float in a 1970s carnival in Penybryn. The sun disappeared and the rain came belting down only to wash the gravy browning off some of their faces. It might have dampened the ground but not the enthusiasm of these wet sun seekers and surfers who are Alison Greenaway, Christopher Shirley, Susan James, Mathew Thomas, Janet Davies, Richard Thomas, Eileen Shirley, Brian Clayton, Michael James.

109. Another fine example of street celebrations for VJ Day, in Brynhuelog Street. It was a fantastic day for the youngsters with plenty to eat and music for everyone. Later most joined up with the residents of Trosnant Street party at the Fox and Hounds. Some of the names are Tresa and Neil Cox, Kenneth and Jan Reynolds, David, Susan Dylan, Gethyn Thomas, Shaun Sharky, Christopher Straten, Ann Marie Lewer, Ian Cox, Julian Spiller, Jean and Chris Lewer, Tracy and Kelly Marie Reynolds, Fay Murphy, Dai and Kath Roberts, Tony and Karen Edwards, Dave and Dot Popadic, Dilwyn and Samantha Reynolds, June Walker, Wayne Evans, Lisa Walker, Huw and Helen Fisher, Catherine and Thomas Fisher, Ton and Carol Sharky, Gareth and Gerwyn Edwards, Ashley Jones, Mark Williams, Shirley Thomas, Charley Lewis, Hansel, Catherine, Allen and Caroline Thomas.

110. An evening out by some of the residents of the Brynheulog Home proved to be a most memorable one. After years of listening to their pop idol, they finally got the chance to see him perform. Pictured here at the home and displaying one of Frankie Vaughan's LP records are, Ron Whitcombe, Terry 'Trousers' Jones, June, Liz Davies Mavis Whitcombe and Mary Jones.

111. Penybryn Blackpool Trip 1940s. Top row: D. Davies, T.J. Jones, C. Hussey, A. Woods, T. Smythe, ? Woods, ?, W. Spiller, ?, W. Williams. Middle Row: ?, M. Davies, R. Pavey, ?, B. Gatfield, ? Woods, ? Christian, ? Smythe, ? Williams, ?, B. Popadic, ? Bottom row: R. Pavey, A. Christian, J. Gatfield, ? Griffiths, V. Woods, O.M. Jones, Mrs. Jones, K. Hussey, ?. Front are Hoteliers.

112. Amongst this picture of some important parliamentarians, led by Prime Minister Tony Blair, is long serving politician Allan Rogers who sits second from the front on the right. Born in Penybryn, Mr. Rogers first joined the Labour Party as a mere 14 year-old and went on to serve in senior positions in Britain and European politics, a career that was long, enduring and eminent; space does not permit the full story unfortunately and an autobiography would be more becoming. After much of a lifetime in the world of politics he retired in 2002 to a more restful existence in Ystrad Mynach.

113. Norman Rogers shown here in this photograph was the Welsh Professional Welterweight Champion. He recalls his days of hard training at the hut in the lane by Cefn Llwyna Farm and sparring with other local boxers such as Pancho Ford and Les Greenaway. The hut was also used for local dances and a base for the Home Guard in which he served. He worked at the Penallta Colliery as a Pit Overman until he left and moved to London in 1960. He now resides in Bournemouth.

114. George and Len Rogers both seen here in uniform in 1943. George in the RAF uniform served in the Dambusters Squadron 617, was awarded the DFC for bravery in the raid on the German battleship *Tirpitz*, he also took part in the Berlin Airlift. Len in the Army uniform served in the commandos during the Second World War, and was involved in rescue work in the Quetta Earthquake. At home he helped in establishing the boxing club in a little hut by Cefn Llwyna Farm.

115. This photograph shows Phil Collins with a Penybryn lad Steve (Pudding) Jones while they were on tour at Lakeland Florida. Steve lived in the prefabs in Gelligaer until he was five, then moved to Penybryn where he attended White City and Gelligaer schools. He worked as a sound engineer for a band called Sassafras and toured the USA several times with the well-known band Jethro Tull. He also worked with various other bands until he got a call from Phil Collins, who was then with Genesis. Steve has worked and toured with Phil for twenty-four years and is now his production manager.

116. These ladies were in charge of the catering arrangements during the opening of Penybryn's Village Hall during the late 1960s. Dot Parker, Peggy Smyth, Harriett Gordon, Mrs. Jones, Doris Reynolds, Brenda Boobier, Phyllis Morris, Heather Partridge, Mrs. Reynolds, Mrs. Silcox, Mrs. Dare, Mrs. Rebecca Quirk, Doreen Thomas, Beryl Rowlands and Muriel Organ.

117. The opening of Penybryn Hall and pictured are Allan Rogers, Ceridwen Rogers, Mrs. Lotte James, Joyce James, John James (Jack), Arthur Skidmore, Mrs. Peggy Skidmore, Mrs. Arthur, Mr. John James, Mrs. Olive James, Mrs. Dacey, Mrs. Evans, Mrs. Kibble, Mr. and Mrs. Christian.

CHAPTER 3

Cascade, Penpedairheol and Glyn-gaer

118. The square Penpedairheol during the time when the village had a Lucarn billiard hall, which had three fine billiard tables. Glyn Lucas later turned this hall into a local butcher's shop, after expanding from the building to the left. Glyn and his wife Brenda ran the shop until his retirement in the 1990s. Another local butcher and farmer Morgan Thomas and family now run the business. The Central Stores owners have been Mrs. Walters, Mrs. Gladys Morgan, Mrs. Olive Jenkins, Mrs. Griffiths, Mike and John Roberts and the current owners are Mark and Andrew Rees.

119. Preparation for building a village hall began in 1952 when a committee was formed and quickly set about raising money. People from the village would buy a brick for a penny and a favourite with the children was the penny ride in an Austin pedal car, from what was known as a ride from White City to the Dyffryn Cottages and back; raffles and donations also helped with the funding. Some members of the committee are pictured here checking on progress of the hall that was situated opposite the Beechgrove Club, Glyn Lucas the local butcher, Molly Holder, George Holder and Mr. Warburton.

120. The first committee of the village hall in Penpedairheol is happy to pose in this 1953 photograph outside the hall. Many people voluntarily helped in this venture that was a great success with a grand opening night with the music provided by Bob Lloyd and his band. At the back are Bert Boulton, Ken Yeo, Ivy Adams, Glyn Harry, Ann Rees, Violet Stevens, Mrs. Sexton, Mr. Warburton, Bulla Horrell, Frank Starr and Cled Williams. The front row is Rose Price, Eva Richards, Glyn Lucas, Sam Davey, George Holder, Mrs. Blodwen Davey, Molly Holder.

121. Every village had a local cobbler's shop and this photograph shows Penpedairheol's. As local shoe and boot repair shop, it was situated at the side of the now local fish shop, with its entrance off Hospital Road. Mr. Sharland ran this repair shop and his son Eddie was later introduced to the business. The cobbler was very much a part of everyone's village life when it was cheaper to have new soles, heels or studs on your shoes than purchase a new pair.

122. The Co-op van was once a familiar sight along our streets in the years before supermarkets were rife and most people having their own mode of transport. The delivery assistants shown here are Mr Perryman, Pat Jenner and Pam Parnell.

123. A sombre funeral procession for eight victims of the Darran Colliery mining disaster in Deri on the morning of 29th October 1909 when twenty-seven miners perished in a very serious explosion underground at the pit. It was said to be the scene of great heroism where five of the rescue team perished. The funeral march is pictured here on Pengam Road Penpedairheol en route to Hengoed Baptist Chapel having walked from Deri.

124. The proprietor of this general store, part of Club Houses poses with his family and shop assistant in this turn-of-the-century photograph. Part of the building was also used as a small village club called the Forestier Walker and was situated on the square Penpedairheol, now the local Post Office, which is run by Jim and Sue Stephens. At the time of this photograph the village Post Office was at 18 Hengoed Road, now the home of Mr. and Mrs. Davey.

125. At one time the Dyffryn Cottages were very isolated, nestling in the dip of Gelligaer and Penpedairheol with the old road winding its way past them; it would have been very picturesque at the time this photograph was taken. Two street names from Dyffryn Parc give us some idea of what the area would have looked like 100 years ago. Nant Y Ffyddlon as pointed out by Iris Evans *'the brook of the faithful'* referring to the Cylla brook where baptisms for Horeb Chapel were given, Maes Y Dderwen *'meadow of oaks'*. In the photograph can be seen Ann Rees, Mrs. Williams with Mrs. Williams's mother in the centre.

126. William George Williams of Pottery Farm Glyn-gaer stands alongside some of his finest Ayrshire dairy cows. William milked all these cows by hand and Mr. Webber from Bargoed, the local milkman was amongst those who received the supply of fresh milk.

127. Farming in the area is demonstrated here with haymaking on what is now Dyffryn Park. Francis Kitt of Cwrt y Betty farm is pictured here with family and friends during the 1950s. The photograph also includes Ronald Kitt, Liz Kitt, Julie Kitt, Helen Kitt, Francis Kitt, Joan Kitt with baby Robert, Maud Kitt.

128. Haymaking on Pottery Farm in the Cwm Cylla valley during the 1950s, when the use of casual labour was customary during the haymaking season. Some of the helpers were miners and some students, with the miners being paid in kind by the farmer. They would be given one or two rows of potatoes in a ploughed field, with the farmer opening and closing the row for them as payment. This was enough to last the miners through the winter. On the cart is Glyn Thomas with Alfred Coles, Ray Exton, Doreen Thomas and Gilmore.

129. Work on Gelligaer Isolation Hospital began in 1911 which was to replace the small and inadequate one at Penybanc in Fochriw, with extensions built in 1922 and 1944. Doctor Bowen Owen was the medical officer and was very well-known in isolating people of the area notably for his efforts in eradicating infectious diseases and visiting schools on a regular basis. Later the hospital beds were given to tuberculosis patients, the premises finally closing in 1973. The photograph includes nurses, doctors, cooks, laundry and domestic staff such as Nan Exton, Val Piper (nee Edmunds), Nel Edmunds, Doctor Bowen Owen, Edna Davies, Miss Grosvenor, Mr and Mrs. Ovens the gardeners, Tom Smith the odd job man, Mr. O'Hagan, Bill Arnott the porter, and Sister Leonard.

130. Photographed in the Hospital grounds these nurses make up the Gelligaer Isolation Hospital Tennis team. With its own courts, tennis was very popular and they had an excellent team, some of the names are - Doreen Halway, Jessie Jones, Margaret Rowlands, Morfa Griffiths, Winnie Evans, Mair Evans, Cath Williams.

131. The relaxed mood of the staff and patients of Gelligaer Isolation Hospital is shown here with these photographs taken on the wards. There were regular fun and games, fancy dress competitions and concerts. The Christmas party was always something special with a lot of hard work going into the Christmas decorations, even the beds had to be decorated. Local jazz bands from Cefn Hengoed, Gelligaer and Gilfach would entertain the patients in the hospital grounds as recalled by Nan and Edna who were former nurses. Nurses Nan Exton (nee Evans), Edna Thomas (nee Davies), Matron Grosvenor, Frances Wilder, Councillor Loveday, Sister Harris, Nurse King, Nurse Roberts, Nurse Duggan, Vera Wild and Mr. Ovens the gardener are amongst the crowd.

132. After lights out the patients would love to hear the funny stories related in the dark by some of the nurses with the odd ghost story told from time to time. The hospital being in a remote place and open to bad weather, the wind would often rattle the old windows and blow down the corridor. The rumour of it being haunted and the strange noises sometimes heard were never explained and the sound of footsteps walking the corridor was always called '*dicky daps*'. Some of the staff and patients are pictured here during one of their entertainment evenings. Nurse Nan Exton nee Evans, Mona Spencer, Vera Wild, Nurse Nancy King, Nurse Stevenson, Sister Leonard, Staff Nurse Wilkins, Edith Pembridge, Nurse Williams, Nurse Price, Sister Chapman, Sister Harris, Daisy Greening, Glenys Davies, Nurse Wallace.

133. The Blackpool outings organised by Dai and Molly Davies were always popular despite the number of hours it took them to reach their destination, still attracting lots of people from the area with regular trips from Cascade, Gelligaer and Penybryn. At this Blackpool Hotel is the Cascade outing together with a few friends from the neighbouring villages. Back: Dai Davies, Mrs. Davies, Dai Kitt, Michael Cushion, ?, Lemual Edwards. Middle: Mr. Woods, ?, Bill and Ivy Adams, ?, Brian Norman, Haydn Adams. Front: Mair Rogers, Ted Jones, Dai Davies, Evelyn Jones, Mrs. Summers, Shirley Norman, Margaret Davies.

134. A great night of laughter and fun for Mrs. McCutcheon's Brownie Pack on Halloween night at Cascade Community Centre in 1988. Some of the pack recalling the fun of making the costumes and trying to make little spiders that most were afraid of even though they were rubber. Top Row: Amy Williams, Catherine Taylor, Lisa Jones, Leanne Jones, ?. Middle Row: ?, Clare Griffiths, ?, Rebecca Williams, Bethan Phillips, Jennifer Williams, Chantel Astley, Alison Mallon, Eleanor Praton, Mrs. McCutcheon. Bottom Row: Nicola Young, Laura Praton, Ceri Jones, Louise Walters, Laura Jenkins, Gemma Chard, Elizabeth Price.

135. This Cascade Juniors A.F.C. 1927-1928 photograph shows one of the old teams of yesteryear and many of the successes of the current village teams have been inspired by the history of football in the area with the skills and know-how being passed down from father to son. Some names known are Bill Morgan and George Callow.

136. It is not certain of the origins of Penpedairheol A.F.C. and how they got their nickname *THE MONSTERS*. Only a few names are known from this 1916-1917 football team and they are John Boyland, Leppo Thomas and John Rees.

137. Cascade Youth Club started in 1967-1968 in the British Legion Club. With no showers and only a tin bath, John Probert and friends quickly set about making the club a success. Although in the early years the teams were often beaten on the field, it wasn't long before the team became Rhymney Valley League and Cup winners, Pontypridd League, East Glam, Gwent League winners and producing three Welsh caps along the way. Those who made the club successful are pictured here along with a 1970s team - Willy Pritchard, Jeff Way, John Probert, Lyn James, Les Holt, Jonathan Rees, Mark Smith, Paul Clabby, Ian Stockdale, Stuart Cook, Steven Mathews, ?, Grant Cushion, Andrew Roberts, Neil Pope, Ian Shepherd, Jason Hughes.

138. Another successful side from Cascade Youth Club from 1982-1983 that added a few more trophies towards the club's reputation of excellence. Neil Coles asst. manager, Dion Jenkins, Sean Baker, David Roberts, Russell Morgan, David Prosser, Geoffrey Bishop, Mike Cushion manager. Front: Kevin Addis, Dean Challenger, Ian Williams captain, Jonathan Rees, Grant Cushion, Dean Davies, Gary Jones. Some achievements are Winners Rhymney Valley League, Runners up Rhymney Valley Cup, Winners Taff Ely Cup, Pontypridd League, Winners Cohen Cup Pontypridd League.

139. Presentation Day and Sports Day are always the highlight of the year and here are the winners with their trophies. ? Roberts, Robert Evans, Ian Shepard, Grant Cushion, Ncil Coles, Gavin Cushion, Adrian Cook, Steven Mathews, Simon Duggan, Scott Rees, Caroline Walker, ?, ? Watkins, Jason Lewis, Tony Wilding, Michael Lewis, ?, Julian James.

140. Much of the Youth Club funds were provided by donations and fundraising and involved a lot of hard work. Marilyn Probert and Mrs. Peggy Hicks are seen here running a tin stall during one of the 1970's carnivals. The proceeds from the stall went towards the mini bus fund that was vital for the club. Both of the ladies were very prominent in the running and organising of fundraising events at the Youth Club.

141. The committee of the Beechgrove Social Club stand alongside the well-known politicians Mr. Allan Rogers and Mr. Ron Davies. The occasion was the official opening of the new hall on 9th December 1982. In the photograph are Mr. Ron Evans, Bill Powell, Mr. Ron Davies, Tom Matthews, Mr. Allan Rogers, Trevor Burke, Keith Parker, Robert Duncan, Johnny *'rock and roll'* Greening, Stan Pope, Billy Rowlands, Dai Price, Jimmy Williams and Mel Jennick.

142. A proud bunch of darters from the Beechgrove Club Penpedairheol, showing off the silverware that they won in this 1965 photograph. The darters are Back: T. Coles, A. Reynolds, B. Reynolds, G. Partridge, S. Eynon, B. Wall, H. Williams, R. Partridge. Seated: Tommy Davies, D. Lewis, G. Williams, W. Pritchard, S. Carter and D. Mathews.

143. The Beechgrove skittles team during the 1980s pictured here on presentation night at the British Legion Club Cascade. A successful year for the lads once again after winning the Pengam and District Summer League seven years out of eight. To be seen are Tony Blewitt, Wyndham Evans, David Price, Stan Carter, Selwyn Davies, Selwyn Jones, Tommy Hayward, Bob Evans, Ray Partridge.

144. The Beechgrove Skittle Team during the early 1970s and proud winners of the Rhymney Valley League after beating the Ex-Servicemen's Club in Bargoed. They went on to represent the Rhymney Valley in the South Wales Championship Clubs Institute Union. In view are Gideon Howells, Brian Davies, Billy Coombes, David Price, Tommy Hayward, Ray Partrige, Id Davies, Granville Dago Davies, Wyndam Mathews, Wilf Snuffy Pritchard, Trevor Carter, Bob Evans, Selwyn Davies, Bill Adams.

77

145. Born in Cascade Penpedairheol Hengoed, Graham Moore went to Glan y Nant Infant's School in Pengam before going to Gilfach Junior and then on to Bargoed Secondary School. He played an active part in all sports playing rugby for his school and becoming junior table tennis champion of the Rhymney Valley. On leaving school at the age of 15 he started work with his father at Penallta Colliery and took up soccer, playing on the wing for Bargoed YMCA. The club helped him on his way to a career in football, and he was always was very appreciative of his days with the Y.M.C.A.. He joined Cardiff City as an amateur and then signed as a professional on his 17th birthday. He won his first Welsh Cap in 1960 at the age of 18 years 224 days, and his last in 1971, with a total of 21 caps and three youth caps for Wales, only the legendary John Charles making his International debut for Wales at a younger age. When Graham left Cardiff in 1961 he first went to Chelsea and

then moved on to Manchester United where he played along side George Best, Denis Law and Bobby Charlton. After leaving Old Trafford he had spells with Northampton, Charlton and Doncaster. One of the highlights of Graham's career was back in 1960 when he scored the goal against Division Two rivals Aston Villa and put Cardiff into the First Division. A crowd of fifty-five thousand watched the match. Here we see Graham with his Empire News Welsh sportsman of the year award 1960.

146. There were celebrations all round for the Gelligaer pony club when they became World Champions at the Mariat Ranch in Virginia U.S.A. in 1982. It was a marvellous achievement for a British team and especially all from the same club. Kevin and Catherine Paynter from Pottery Farm Glyn-gaer have a history of winning championships both as a team and as individuals. Their home has many trophies, whether it's the Royal Welsh or the UK Championship they can compete with the best. An outstanding achievement by Kevin was when he became the M.G.A.G.B. World Champion three years in succession, the first person to achieve this award and with this achievement he was allowed to keep the cup. Some of the finest examples of Welsh ponies are to be found at the farm namely the Cwm Cylla Stud and are breeding for temperament and performance. The team were Kevin and Cathryn Paynter, Ken Paynter (Trainer), Jamie Duggan, Phillip ? and Jane Yeoman.

147. A British Legion Outing photograph that captures some of the following ladies - Mrs. Richards, Brenda Willetts, Mrs. Lambley, Mrs. Farmer, Mrs. Bartlett, Mrs. Osbourne, Mrs. Stevens, Eileen Williams, Mrs. Cox, Mrs. Christopher, Margaret Parnell, Ruth Trivett, Mrs Bishop, Mrs Morgan (Taxi).

148. A group of sportsmen from the British Legion Club in Cascade poses for this photograph in 1962, after winning the Rhymney Valley Darts League. In the group are Jim Pipe, Ken Davies, David Williams, Bill Jennick, Tommy James, Brian Webber, Bill Sopper, Dai Lewis, Tommy Jenkins, Billy Coombes, Tucker Munslow, Ray Price, Gwillym Wallbank, Clive Edwards, Bill Duncan, Edwin Piper, Gareth Williams, Harry Smith, Kenny Gingell and Johnny Sinnet.

149. This time it's the turn of Pendarren Street Cascade who are always very enthusiastic for any street party or carnival that is taking place in the village. Here we have some of the residents and their names are Nell Edwards, Carol Adams, Graham Hughes, Alan Jones, Etty Jones, Sandrina Wilcox, Gwyneth Addis, Mrs. Roberts, Megan Thomas, Gladys Clabby, Glenys Hughes, Molly Holder, Jean Jenkins, Mrs. Kerslick, Pat Clabby, Vernon Clabby, Sally Jones, Ron Griffiths, Beryl Griffiths.

150. As part of the Jubilee celebrations of 2002, the Casc-Aid Carnival produced some wonderful floats and was a tribute to the committee that had worked so hard over the year to stage the event. Glyn-gaer version of Sister Act was full of fun, singing and laughter and won rapturous applause from all the spectators. The players are Carol Evans, Jackie Hopkins, Diane Cooper, Pat Gorham, Ursula Atkinson, Star Hurcombe, Linda McCarthy, Joyce Evans, Louise Evans, Val Evans, Jan Denham, Barbara Jennick and Dai Hopkins.

151. The Cascade and Penpedairheol Carnival Queen along with the pageboys and girls are photographed here on the Dyffryn fields in 1954 following the success of the Coronation Queen the year before. Seen are Joyce Bayliss, ?, David Hammer, Sandra King, Eileen Davey (Carnival Queen who later became Miss TV Rhymney Valley), Evan Holifield, Enid Rees, Phyllis Horrell, Valerie Edmunds.

152. The cowboy, cowgirl and Indian outfits were always favourite Christmas presents, with the extras like gun and holster, bow and arrow and the Indian tent they made the perfect gift. These outfits were put to good use in this 1950s carnival in Cascade. Just turning off Pengam Road is this splendid float with Alun Thomas, Nova Smith, Lyn Jones, (Buster) and Sue Stevens.

153. To celebrate the Coronation of the Queen in 1953 the residents of Cascade and Penpedairheol chose Mrs. Eva Richards as their Carnival Queen. Here are some residents of the village who played the Carnival Queen with her royal court. Pictured in the grounds of Cascade Baptist Chapel are, Iris Christopher, Mrs. Roberts, Molly Holder, Mrs. Sexton, Mrs. Christopher, Jean Thomas and Miss Thomas, Mrs. Rogers, Mrs. Eva Richards and Megan Thomas.

154. Some of the onlookers who had witnessed the above photographic session taking place decided to have their photograph taken following the departure of the Carnival Queen. They are Billy Cowles, John Thomas, Mr. And Mrs. Len Moore, Betty Stevens, Mrs. Thomas Lucas, Mrs. Davies, Charlie Bishop, Mr. and Mrs. Baz Lewis, Mrs. Davey, Mrs Kitty, Mrs. Warn, Mrs. Hayle, Mr. Willets, Mrs. Vi Williams top street.

155. 1969 was a great year for the Cascade carnival and making its way up Pengam Road is the Winter Wonderland float with Linda Griffiths as Snow Queen, the Carnival Queen float is seen just in front. On the float are Linda Griffiths, Lisa Warburton, Julie Rothwell, Velina Warburton, Tina Warburton, Trudy Jones, Phillip Wilcox, Rosena Rothwell, Barbara Hughes, Sheila Smith, Wayne Smith, Gwyneth Addis.

156. Although only a few names are known of the group being made up of Lillian Mills and her pack of Brownies and Guides, it looks like they are set to cause mayhem, as they become the girls of St. Trinians for the day in this 1979 carnival. Lillian who was captain for 14 years, recalls some of the fun of the organisation, with the camp outings to Tal-y-Bont, Dan-yr-Ogof with pony trekking, the camp fires and sing-along and fancy dress nights all just part of the fun; on 'Dick the farm's' cattle wagon everyone piled on and had a good laugh. The toilet tent was quite funny when one saw the portal potty and asked where is the flush. A special mention must be made of Gladys Griffiths captain of Hengoed Guides for her role in promoting the organisation in the valley.

157. An early photograph of the Plough and Harrow public house which is situated on the square Penpedairheol. The pub's suppliers of their ales and stouts were Webbs of Aberbeeg and were well known for their fine brews. Note the St. John Ambulance shed to the right of the photograph.

158. With Italy making up the Six Nations Rugby championships there is never any shortage of supporters willing to make the trip to Rome. Duncan Stonelake landlord of the Plough is seen here with some of the regulars just before their trip in 2001. Eager to try out the delights of Rome's finest restaurants of spaghetti, pasta and pizza and not forgetting a sample of their ales, are Steve Carter, Kerry Grisley, Nigel Davies, Duncan Stonelake, Geoff Simmons, Dai Roberts and Vince Brown.

159. The Scotland trip is always a favourite with Welsh rugby supporters and pictured here are the Plough and Harrow regulars just about to make their way to the waiting bus. Smiling for the camera are, back row - John Probert, Robert Evans, Howard Pritchard, Johnny Rupnick, John Cobley, Billy Hill, Dai Davies and Malcolm Tucker. Middle row - Ian Llewellyn, Ian Horrell, Mike Hamer, Howard Barstaple, John Richards, Nayo Greenaway, Noel Woods and Tony Redford. Front row - Vernon Powell, Trevor Whatley, Doug Horrell, Dai Hopkins, Arthur Postians and Dai Barstaple.

160. A float from Glyngaer makes its way past the Plough in the Millennium Carnival. The king is Peter Davey, the teacher Jane Probert and prince Cairion Evans. The pupils are Zara Partis, Casey Evans, Caris Humphries, Melvin Humphries, Jodi, Jade, Liam and Joshi Probert, Rhianna Davies, Amber ?, Charlotte ?, Luke Clark, Lauren Thomas.

161. This was the first Christmas party after the opening of Cascade and Penpedairheol Village Hall in 1953. It was a tremendous success for the organisers and had to be split into two sessions. To be seen are Cled Williams, Pauline Pipe, Wendy Roberts, Cynthia McIntosh, Edna Summers, Nova Smith, Lorraine Kitt, Diana Kitt, Mrs Yeo, Mrs. Duncan, Harry Smith, Mrs. Lovell, Pat Moore, Jennifer King, Mrs. Young, Mrs. Stevens, Mrs. Cushion, Robert Davey, Mrs. Kitt, Mrs. Williams, Olwen Cowles, Molly Holder, Vi Stevens, Janette Smith, Jennifer Holt, Ann Greyson, Betty Hollifield, Terrence Cushion, Marilyn Bridgway, Diane Thomas, Lesley Rugmai, Sheila Summers, Alan Thomas, Pat Sage, Richard Hollifieid, John Thomas, Jeanette Smith, Bernard Stephens, Rosemary Sage.

162. What a wonderful turnout for this senior citizens outing to Belgium in the 1980s, that was made up of people from around the area. Bert and Gertie Smith, Bill and Ivy Adams, Bill and Margaret Williams, Stuart and Violet Stevens, Flo Basset, Mrs. Molly Davies, Bill and Maisie Ennis, Maggie Lewis, Dilwyn and Olive Davies, Trevor and Myrtle Carter, Mrs. Violet Evans, Mr. and Mrs. Pipe, Eunice Evans, Mrs. Middleton, Mrs. Muriel Arthur, Idris Rawlings, Gwen Rawlings, Bill Elms, Mr. Smith, Mrs. Piper, Mrs. Lambley, Mrs. Chipperfield, Mrs. Evans, Mr. Sinet, Margaret Parnell, ? Thomas, Mrs. Bassett, Bill Bishop, Margaret Lewis, Jane Jones, Mary ?, John and Olive James, Maynard Phillips, Mary Phillips, Fred Rawlings, Nan Rawlings, Mrs. Lambley, Mrs Bishop, Mr. And Mrs. Spencer, Mr. And Mrs. David Evans, Mrs. Poyntz, Alice Evans, Mrs. Davies, Mr.and Mrs. David.

163. Many of trips were run from Cascade village and pictured here was one to Porthcawl during the 1930s; John Rees and Gerald King were the organisers with many of the older residents of the village still recalling those happy events of summer outings. The charabanc being the only mode of transport and there were always at least two or three from each village. The helter skelter to the left of the photograph was one of the prominent shows at funfairs. Megan and Nancy Rees, Bessie Lewis the shop, the Partridge family, John Rees, Gerry Morgan and his father, Mr. and Mrs. Bob Jones and family, Haydn Morgan, Tommy Duffy Williams are amongst the trippers.

164. The hire of fancy dress costumes was unheard of when these fine examples of outfits were made for a 1950s carnival in Cascade. The simplicity of the little boy being shipwrecked adds to the photograph and the fun of making your own costume and making all laugh with delight. Some names are Peter Carter, Doug Smith, Haydn Adams, Maureen O'Hagan, Terry Davies, Evan Hollifield, Maggie Lewis and the Davies family from Gilfach, the Langford family from Pengam.

165. A Cascade resident Molly Holder is pictured here with the famous singing duo from the seventies, Peters and Lee. They were just two of the many artistes who stayed at Molly's house for a night or two while touring and playing the clubs in the area. Molly was always at the heart of the action whether it was the involvement of the building of the first community centre to an active part in the running of the hall.

166. The Royals Jazz Band was formed in 1994 as a result of some girls having a laugh during a bus journey to work. During their first year they won the National Indoor Championships. In the picture are Liam Richards on the drum with Gavin Williams, Susan Harris and Sheryl Scanlon the trainer.

167. Children of Bryncoed. Andrew Thomas, Mathew Thomas, Hazel Thomas, Lynda Thomas, Helen Thomas, Allan Williams, Lisa Williams, Karen Fieldhouse, Christopher Fieldhouse, Darren Taylor, Michael Vick, Joseph Pope, Wayne Pope, Nicky Pope, Carina Walker, Jason ?, Ian Bond, Mark Bond, Michelle Bond, Sharon ?, Mary Welsh, Pat Paterson, Peter Paterson, June Paterson, Cheryl Paterson, M. Walker, Lynette Roberts, Michael Roberts, Jamie ?, and in the background is Mrs. Davey.

168. To celebrate the opening of the Village Hall in 1953 the organisers put on a dance with Bobby Lloyd and his Band from Gelligaer. In the picture are Trevor Christopher, Trevor Price, Bill Horrell, Bert Boulton, Ken Yeo, Ralph Watson, Rose Price the matron of Gelligaer Hospital, Bill Cowles, Evelyn Cushion, Eddie Yeo, Molly Holder, Leyton Rees, George Holder, Mrs Davies, Mrs. Sexton,Vi Stevens, Blodwen Davey.

169. The Cascade Fairies photographed in the 1950s of the Methodist Chapel in the village are seen here in a play. The Chapel was built in 1929 by Britains of Fleur De Lys. Much of the money raised was by fundraising, donations and buying a brick for a few pennies. Included in the picture are Liz McQue, Cynthia Stevens, Jean Holt, June James. Shirley Holt, Betty Holifield, Julia Northcote, Sharon O'Hagan, Lynda Holt, Jackie Parry, Joyce Trivett.

170. Some of the early members of the Cascade, Penpedairheol and Glyn-gaer carnival committee pictured here on the Welfare Ground field. Eddie Young, Mrs. Stonelake (Mrs. Christopher), Mrs. Thomas, Mrs. Stevens, Mr and Mrs. Derek, Mr. Moore, Mrs. Bishop, Mrs. Bolton, Grace Owen, Mrs. Partridge, Mrs. Bartlett, Ivy Adams, Mr. Pipe, Ossie Kitt, Mr. Lewis, Mrs. Sexton, Mrs. Blatchford, Mr. Christopher, Frank Loveday, Mrs. Bishop, Mr. Partridge are to be seen.

171. Many people will recall the carnivals of the 1970s and 80s and would remember some of the people involved in the splendid variation of floats. Pictured here are some of the members of the carnival committee that was responsible for its existence today. Nell Edwards, Vera Hughes, Betty Vick, Gwen Smith, Gaynor Carter, Ann Jones, Hilary De La Taste, Christine Thomas, Beryl Griffiths.

172. 'Hands off our allotments' the placards read and this is what the group of demonstrators was trying to do to the property developers. During the 1980s and 90s housing estates were being built around Hengoed Road and with that, the threat of losing their allotments. After a successful campaign the area was saved from being lost to the village and is now producing some of the finest produce in the country. The demonstrators in the photograph are Ken Davey, Marjorie Coombes, Bill Coombes, Bill Soper, Jim Pipe, Granville Davies, Johnny Horne, Selwyn Jones, Mrs. Jones, with Glyn Whitcombe recording the event.

173. The Cascade Allotments Association has had a remarkable history since it was formed during the 1970s. The standard and quality of its fruit, vegetables and flowers has exceeded beyond all expectations, producing Welsh, British and National champions in all its classes. In the picture are Mr. Bodman, Mike Davies, Roy Tudor, Paul Bodman, Barbara Parker, Jen Jenkins and Jim Thomson.

174. The families of Hengoed Road are pictured here during the street party celebrations of 1953. Many people remember those fantastic carnivals and parties of that year and Hengoed Road's contribution is an example of the team spirit that they had. Some of the events of that day are featured in this book, with the crowning of the Carnival Queen in the grounds of the village chapel. The families are Gwen Lewis and either Keith or Robert as a baby, Theresa Evans, Vi Evans, Thelma Hinton and baby Joy Hinton, Tootsie Boulton, Jean Jones, Cheryl Callow, Barbara Sharp and the children of the Richards family and Lucas family.

175. During the 1970s there were many carnivals in Cascade and Penpedairheol and here is one float from Hengoed Road. There was never any shortage of flatbed lorries supplied by Robert Lewis Haulage for the floats, but on the day, Roger Carter kindly lent this small one. The carnival float was made up from the following - Robert Lewis, Anna Lewis, Jane Lewis, Lesley Derrick, Sylvia Derrick, Maria Derrick, Andrew Derrick, Andrea Harding, Dawn Smith and the master of wizardry Keith Derrick.

176. The late Bert Evans of Glyn gaer is photographed here in the back garden of his house in Oxford Street. On leaving the army he worked as a bus driver until his retirement, his love for buses fuelled his hobby of collecting bus memorabilia and together with his son Robert built up a remarkable collection. He was a member of the Cascade Pigeon Club and he was overjoyed when he won the Lerwick race with one of his birds.

177. Behind the bar and at your service at the Plough and Harrow was Jeanne Hill of Penpedairheol. With over thirty years service at the pub, she waved goodbye to four of the landlords. Whilst reminiscing Jeanne remembers the 'go as you please' nights and the sing along with Haydn Briggs on piano, John Probert on washboard and Harry Grant on bass.

178. The White City pirates might have sailed the seven seas in the hope of finding the odd cargo ship to rob or even hunt for Blackbeard's treasure at Barry Island. On this particular day in 1969 during the Investiture celebrations, they were about to challenge a team of girls from Gelligaer in a fancy dress football match. David Hurcombe Adele Holt, Barbara Jennick, John Pope, Lorraine Williams, Ann Meredith, Lorraine nee Baines, Pat Goram.

CHAPTER 4

The Welfare Ground

179. The Gelligaer Welfare Ground is situated between the villages of Penpedairheol, Glyn Gaer and Gelligaer, and there have been many sporting events and carnivals on its fields. It was known for many years as White City Welfare Ground. The long sporting history of the area has benefited the youngsters today, and is shown in this last section of the book. The views shown are of Glyn Gaer (White City) and the Welfare Ground is to the left of the picture. The village and school (built in 1914) are to the right.

180. Many of the residents will recall the open fields that were teaming with wildlife in this photograph of what is now Forest Park. Susan Evans is pictured here as she strolls around these fields in this 1960s photograph. The villages of Glyn Gaer (White City) and Castle Hill Gelligaer are seen in the distance. Some residents still refer to the road leading up to Gelligaer as the new road. Although work began in the late 1930s, it was not completed until the 1940s, it being shelved due to the outbreak of war. Spectators would have a spectacular view of the welfare ground from this road prior to the obstruction of trees.

181. Over the past 64 years Gelligaer Bowls Club has a history to be proud of with many of the original founder members' families involved at the club today. The club was formed in 1938 and has many league titles to its name. The ladies section was formed in 1986 and has contributed to the club's exceptional record of success with league titles of their own. Some of the original members are pictured here in this Rhymney Valley League winner's photo of 1948. J. Davies, R. Sloggett, G. Roberts, E.J. Hughes, S. Lewis, S. Holder, T. John, A.V. Thomas, H. Surridge, R. Williams, H. Martin, F. Bray, J. Turner (Chairman), E. Williams, E. Bickham, W.S. Bishop (secretary), I. Davies, F. Rice (treasurer), Fk. Rice, E. Holt, W. Roberts, E. Hole, B. Lewis.

182. Another successful Gelligaer Bowls team, this time from the 1980s with Simon Elias, Keith Dalton, David Elias, George Banks, Jack Rees, Graham Partridge, Bob Evans, K.Griffiths, Gwyn Jones, Derek Lewis, Graham Williams, Ron Partridge, Harry Martin, Tyrone Rowlands, Haydn Jennick, John Dacey, Mike Meredith, Bill Williams, Bill Price, Selwyn Jones, Bill Banks, Tony Cusack, Paul Jenkins, Gareth Meredith.

183. This large gathering of the Gelligaer Bowls team members was for the occasion of the opening of the new clubhouse in 2001. The club was officially opened by Mr. Graham Court O.B.E. accompanied by his wife Pearl. The members and guests present in this photograph are Jan Chandler, Silvia Derrick, Rosemary Jones, Howard Thomas, Gareth Meredith, Gwyn Lewis, Bob Evans, Alan Lewis, Tony Cusack, Paul Hemmings, Ray Partridge, Gwyn Jones, Darren Puddyfoot, Tommy Hill, Steve Gorham, Gareth Williams, Peter Bufton, Mel Vick, Lenny Holton, David Williams, Tommy Pritchard, John Charles, Michael Meredith, Granville Boyland, Andy Coombes, Ray Goodland, Dennis Cousins, Haydn Warburton, Brian Adams, Colin Adams, Jill Court, Rita Moyle, Yvonne Bufton, Pat Gorham, Margaret Berrett, Councillor Graham Court O.B.E. Idris Owen, County Councillor Keith Derrick, Gwyn Phillips, Ponty Jones, Austin Jones, Eileen Jones, Pat Lewis, Maureen Puddyfoot, Mary Palmer, Heather Hill, Pat Williams, Lillian Adams, Rita Iles, Betty Williams, June Cousins, Jean Parry (ladies county president), Keith Dalton (secretary), Paul Jenkins (chairman), Megan Boyland, Marlene Jones, Sheila Hemmings, Jean Towell, Graham Gibbs.

184. A fine photograph of the Gelligaer and District rugby team of 1932-33. The names are M. Birt, S. Rosser, S. Tingle, W.H. Williams, W. Lewis, J. Harrigan, I. Davies, P. Price, E. Walters, D.O. Williams, A. Evans, L. Moore, B. Jones, L. Ennis, T. Keen, W. Kitt, D. Prosser, P. Gane, R. Thomas (Trainer), I.J. Walters (Treasurer), O. Kitt, J. Stonelake, D.C. Jones (Capt), F. Kitt, T. Coles, W.J. Rees (Sec), J. Evans, D. Kitt, T. Watkins, H. Archer (Chairman), M. Jones.

185. Gelligaer football team in the 1920s. Back: M. Birt, J. Richards, E. Jones. Upper middle: J. Lewis, (Treas.), W.J. Rees (Sec.), D. Jones, W.H. Kitt, A. Ingram, T. Holt, W. Jones, D. Murphy (Chairman), T. Holt Snr. Lower middle: R. Hooker, J. Coombes, Mrs. J. Lewis (Pres), T. Evans, J. Ennis. Front: W. Evans, T. Williams.

186. Cascade Youth Club football team 1996-97. Back Row: Ivan Hill (Midland Bank manager), Keith Down, David Edwards, Eurig Bowen. Middle Row: Gary Davies, Ian Dillon, Christopher Hopkins, David Williams, Michael Edwards, Robert Franklin, Mathew Lewis, Anthony Berry. Front Row: Gareth McCarthy, Lee Davies, Paul Evans, Marcus Edwards, Tony Price, Kevin Downs, Huw Bowen, Glen Spearey, Jamie Cotter. Cascade Youth Club opened at the Welfare Ground in 1996 and has continued the standard of football played by the teams. The under 13s 1996-97 and Rhymney Valley Cup Winners are a tribute to all the staff at the club who worked so hard in its setting.

187. Cascade Youth Club Under 16s 2001-02. The club's football teams have excelled themselves with both the U12s and U16s becoming league and cup champions. Pictured here are the U16s who have done the double three years out of four. They are Ffloyd Williams, Mathew Stephens, Alex Langford, Luke Franklin, Keiron Mahoney, Marc Cochran, Phillip Bishop, Chris Gatefield, Lee Miles, Dion Jenkins (Manager), Lloyd Grist, Adam Pearce, Luke Collins, Anthony Jenkins, Tom Gorham, Leon Young, André Soroko, Mathew Hutcheon, Robbie Davies and Michael Hopkins.

188. Gelligaer Cricket 1936. Mr. Poulson, Jim Turner the grave digger, Stan Holder, Edgar Davies, Tommy Druney, ?, Bill Davies, David Rees Jones, Ivor Davies, Sergeant Williams, Tommy Richards, Les Poulson, Glyn Price, Mr. Loveday chairman of the council, Bill Exton, Glyn Davies, Idris Davies and Canon J.O. Williams.

189. Gelligaer Welfare Cricket Team 1950s. G. Thomas, T. Richards, Les Poulson, J. Howells, G. Davies, T. Frowen, T. Holder, G. Goldsworthy, K. Lloyd, Idris Davies, Ken Thomas, G. Price, Bill Exton, Arthur Callow, Norman Jones.

CHAPTER 5

Schooldays in the District

190. Gelligaer School Top Row: Raymond King, Billy Underwood, John Sinnett, Michael Vallance, ? Marsden, Bertie Wittock, Donald Rees, David Jenkins, Colin Morgan, Gwyn Evans, ?. Next Row Johnny Forward (Headmaster), ?, Jeannette Batholomew, Elizabeth Silvier, Marlene Fowler, Sheila Fletcher, Pat Harrigan, Florence Jones, Bernice Fewings, Pat Doloway, ? Pritchard. Next Row: Marilyn Arthur, Marlene Moses, Margaretta Greening, ?, Jean Richards, Sadie Phillips, Eileen Lewis, Phyllis Horrel, Myra Rice, P. Jones, ?. Bottom Row: Clive Evans, David Lewis, Graham Davies, ?, ?, Gerald Woods, Clive Howard.

191. Gelligaer School 1940s. Top row: K. Price, D. Murphy, S. Davies, D. Thomas, D. Rees, M. Williams, N. Reakes, S. Brake, A. Whitefoot. Middle row: Headmaster J . Forward, T. Arthur, R. Davies, T. Jenkins, A. Williams, V. Silcox, G. Jones, P. Hill, T. Jones, G. Tucker, D. Lewis, D. Osbourne, Miss Jesse Coles class teacher. Bottom row: A. McCarthy, P. Palmer, B. Reynolds, V. Bickham, V. Rogers, M. Evans, L. Underwood, T. Morris, K. Greaney, E. Quirk.

192. Gelligaer School 1959. Top: Mrs. Williams, Trevor Burke, Michael Shelton, Keith Parker, Brian Mathews, Paul Garett, Gareth ?, Desmond Parry, Colin Gilbert, Dilwyn Parker. Middle: Graham Morris, Cynthia McIntosh, Sandra Davies, Janet Morgan, ?, Jean Paget, Lorraine Kitt, Donald McAlpine, Kenny Moses, David Evans, Johnny Forward (Head Teacher). Lower: Julie Lewis, Mary Evryn, Jean Pritchard, Maureen Clifford, Glynis Jenkins, Hilary Paget, Gillian Arthur, Carol Jenkins, Lillian Skidmore, Rosemary Smith. Floor: Tyrone Morgan, Gareth Bray, David Baines.

193. Gelligaer Village School. John Exton, Linda Boobier, Lyndon Boobier, Mansel Jones, John Exton, Geoffrey Meyrick, Alan Osborne, Paul Clyburn, George Bettinson, Andrew Padfield, Howard Padfield. Barry Jones, ?, Suzanne Gillard, Sheryl Palmer, Kay Harding, Maria Burton, Gillian Kitt, Pamela Lewis, Helen Wood, Lance Phillips, Jacqueline ?, Julie Derrick, ?, Julie Lewis, Sandra Rees, June Harris, ?, Rosemary Price, Julia Thomas, ?. Michael Partridge, ? Pritchard, Glen Murphy, Alan Hopkins, Phillip Cartwright, Clive Jones, ?, Jeffrey Owen.

194. Gelligaer Welsh Girls in the school yard with the Harp Inn in the background. Linda Broughton, Mary Bettinson, Carol Jenkins, Susan Organ, ?, Sandra Davies, Lillian Skidmore, Wendy McCarthy, Wendy Bray, Marina Davies, ?, ?, Marina Parry, Maria Popadic, Marilyn Jones, Jean Caswell.

195. Welsh Girls Gelligaer School 1963-64 which includes ? Pritchard, Susan Powell, Hayley Norman, Joy Lynch, Julie Jones, Janet Holder, Annette Bengough, Margaret Powell, Sharon Gibb, Wendy Gilbert, Miriam Greening, Ann Jenkins, Catherine Thomas, Susan Bray, Kathryn Benson, Susan Jenkins, Sheila Rowlands.

196. Gelligaer School 1959-60. Hywell Jones, Cliff Pritchard, Morris McCarthy, Howard Pritchard, Paul Darch, Clive Jones, Paul Harris, Alan Denham, Johnny Forward, Glyn Davies, Graham Woods, Brian Gordon (skippy), Eirion Gatefield, Pam Martin, ?, Ross Evans, Carl Ackerman, Dave Thomas, Alan Price. Irene Smith, Mary Bettinson, Pam Harris, ? Davies, Sandra Morris, ?, ?, Gaynor Garbutt, Susan Organ, Kathy Burke.

197. Gelligaer School 1960s. Mr. Browning, Mark Bettinson, ?, Steve Jones, Gary Speary, ? Wilfred Mathews, Gareth Hopkins, Stuart Chard, Richard Melbey, Alan Wild, Mrs. Williams. Johnny Hennygan, Keith Powell, Robert Jenkins, Graham Morgan, ?, Sandra Haydn, Jennifer Marsden, Dilip Lalwan, Brian Clifford, Susanne Davies, Margaret Thomas, Carol Adams, Sylvia Norman, ?, Margaret Skidmore, Janet Sheperdson, ?, Linda Carter, Robert Evans Billy Gordon, Robert Jones.

198. Gelligaer village school non-teaching staff 1970s. Many readers will remember these familiar faces of Gelligaer village school and many recalling the walk from their school to another for dinners. Mrs. Nan Exton, Glenys Davies, ?, Peggy Thomas, Lynda McMarthy, Barbara Williams, Gwen Gibbs, Muriel Jones, Mrs. A. Jones, Gwen ?, Mrs. Ashton.

199. Gelligaer School 1950s. Teachers Mr. Browning and Mrs. Joyce Walters. Top Row: Alan Boulton, Mike Davies, ?, Kenny Reynolds, David Clark. Middle Row: Michael Reeks, Dilwyn Parker, Elizabeth Kitt, Sandra Davies, Wendy McCarthy, Eirion Gatefield, Greg Lucas. Bottom Row: J. Lewis, Sherrie Rogers, Rhonwen Jenkins, Janet Davies, Lillian Skidmore, Myrtle Lewis, June Pritchard, Mariana Davies, Lionel Pritchard, Terry Morris.

200. Gelligaer Village School in the 1960s with Melvyn Pearce, ?, Keith Osborne, Theresa Whittle, Sharon Young, Kathrine Lockyear, Phillip Morgan, Meirion Edwards, Phillip Baines, Mr. Jones form Teacher. ?, Wayne Huxtable, Clive Young, Lyn Rees, Lyn Exton, Craig Phillips, ?, Frank Kitt, Steven Evans, Phillip Rowlands, Barry Jones, ?, Cathy Murphy, Kim Jones, Josephine Frowen, Sharon Franklin, Carol Anstell, Carol Amos, ?, ?, ? Clark, Clive Cartwright, Lee Jones Gary Davies, Phillip Woods.

201. Included in this school picture from 1953-54 are Jeff Rees, R. Evans, Brian McCarthy, Cyril Davies, Terence Lynch, John Stevenson, Desmond Willetts, Rosmond Herbert, Jean McAlpine, David Cooper, Dennis Lynch, Joyce Maloney, Dawn Carter, Mary Miles, Lynette Pritchard, Celia Brake, Nova Chard and Sherry Reynolds.

202. Gelligaer village school 1970s with Raymond Norman, Andrew Cartwright, Jeff Gifford, ? Hollifield, ?, Wayne Chabling, Mark Bailey, John Price, David Jenkins, Gerald Haydn, Steven Jenkins, Kenneth Cattle, Terry Wild, Richard Dollaway, ?, Robert Courts, Jeff Sharp, Alison Bryce, Lynnette Moon, Cathleen Davies, Christine Davies, Mr. Wynn David (Head Teacher), Collette Baker, Trena Ellis, Alan Jenkins

203. Some of the teachers and schoolchildren of Gelligaer Village School dressed up for St Davids Day 1971. Mrs. Myrtle Owen (Headmistress), Mr. Hywel Jones (Deputy Head), Mr. Wynn David, Lyndon Jenkins, Gina Thomas, Anne S. Jones, Mrs. Blatchford, Anwen Edwards, Collette House, Ann Bingham, Maria Price, Julie Forest, Margaret Rees, Angela Rose, Siân Thomas, Miss E. Davies, Mrs. N. Adams, Pamela Dobbins, Julie Griffiths, Cerri Evans, Deborah Thomas, Dominique Rose, Jane Jennick, Wendy Gilbert, Clare Clark, Pat Fowler and Tanya ?. Also pictured are two girls by the name of Debbie Davies!

204. Gelligaer Village White City School about 1956. Top: Kenny Davies, David Pearce, Brian Morgan, John Murphy, Kenny Davies, Michael Hickie, John Davies, Nigel Palmer, Mrs Bevan (Teacher), Andrew Morris. Middle: Gareth James, Craig Griffiths, Wendy Davies, Michael Munslow, ?, ?, Marilyn Jones, Peter Reynolds. Bottom: ?, Gail Richards, ?, ?, Linda Parker, Teressa Donnan, Annette Morris, Maria Popadic, ?, ?, ?.

205. Gelligaer Village Juniors 1980s. Teacher, Clare Morgan, Lisa Jones, Lee Woods, Louise Chapman, Clare Webb, Leanne Barker, Donna Pritchard, Bethan Pope, Mrs. Griffiths. Mrs. Higgins, Catherine Taylor, Donna Kinsgley, Rachel Mathews, Lisa Pritchard, Leanne Jones, Roshan ?, Cheryl Williams, Donna Ennis, Vera Griffiths, Emma Clements, Steve Jones, Teacher Christine Morgan, Mrs. James (Head Teacher). Leon Hall, Leigh Morris, Mark Andrews, Paul Emmanuel, Craig Kinsgley, Daniel Jones, Michael Carlick, Russell Maloney, Robert Shutt, Gavin Jones, John Thomas, Wayne Thomas. David Roberts, Mark Evans, Elinor Pratten, Laura Davies, Clare Griffiths, Steve Blewett, John Blewett, Charles Underwood, David Pugh.

206. Gelligaer Village Junior School 1991-92. The pupils and teachers of Gelligaer Village Junior School folk dancing team during a 'Day of Dance' organized by the school. The team toured all around the villages performing to the enjoyment of everyone who came out to see them. The folk dancing team later performed at the National Eisteddfod at Ebbw Vale. Rachel ?, Barry Hamer, Mathew Carlick, Kevin Rees, Andrew Fursland, Gareth Coles, Mathew Thomas, Oliver Carroll, David Boucher, Andrew Peters, Andrew Griffiths, Rebecca Williams. Sali Davies, Alison Malon, Eleanor Whiteman, Teresa Edmunds, Carly Rees, Catherine Thompson, Laurie Jenkins, Jennifer Davies. The teachers are Mrs. Margaret Gwenlan, Mrs. Karen Jones and Mrs. Marian Whiteman.

207. Gelligaer Village School 1990s. Kayleigh Phillips, Dwayne Greenway, Lee Davies, ?, Kate Atkinson, Jonathan Davies, Jonathan Cartwright, Anthony Brooks. Michelle Taylor, Rebecca Engwell, Rebecca Prosser, Nathan Thomas, ?, Rhys Cochran, Michelle ?, Rachel Hawker, ?, Laura Simmons, James Mathews, Samantha Whatley, Liam Richards, Nerys Robinson, Thomas Powell, Amy Evans, ?. Teachers Julie Roberts and Debbie ?.

208. Gelligaer Village Juniors Netball Team 'A' champions of 1997. It's all smiles for these youngsters as they display their shield and trophies and it's another success for Mrs Grmusa's team and the school. Jennifer Williams, Emma Hopkins, Kate Davies, Joanne Jenkins, Mrs. Grmusa, Janine Lewis, Joanne Mcarthy, Joanne Lewis.

209. Gelligaer Village School sports has excelled over the years with a growing number of talented sports children. The school's rugby team has gone from strength to strength and achieved some remarkable results. They were winners of the Ford Dragon Rugby Extravaganza 2000 and have some promising players for the future. One such player is Lucas Edwards pictured here with the team, he was chosen to carry the Welsh flag in the opening and closing ceremonies of the Rugby World Cup at the Millennium Stadium in 1999. Team members are Kyle Burgess, David Quartermain, Gerwyn Edwards, Owain Williams, Lee Davies, Geraint Morris, Nathan Mahoney, Nathan Lydster, Lucas Edwards, Ceri Jones.

210. Gelligaer schools football 1939-1940. Mr. Johnny Forward, Harold Davies, C. Tucker, Doug Rees, Des Rees, Ted Double, Alf Jones, K. Franklin, Mr. Dago (Head Teacher). Wyndam Boobier, Wilf Mathews, Henry Wakley, Tubby Smerton, Oliver Pritchard.

211. Gelligaer School Rugby 1932-33. Teachers are Johnny Forward, A. Hughes, Mr. Owen, Mr. Jones. Top row, ? Jones, Theo Sinclair, ?, Tucker Pritchard, Berty Mitchell, Ray Davies. Middle row, W. Wheelan, Les Poulson, ?, Glyn Davies, Arthur Callow, ?, ?. Bottom row, R.O. O'Hagan, Norman Rogers, ?, W. Birt, A. Smith.

212. Gelligaer Village Junior and Primary School Teachers 2002. Mr. Gordon Dey, (caretaker), Mrs. Yvonne Lever, Miss Leanne Pritchard, Mrs. Jeanette Lloyd, Mrs. Gillian Fisher, Miss Jane Evans, Mrs. Angela Grmusa, Mrs. Pamela Jenkins, Mrs. Hazel Minney, Mrs. Pauline Cooling, Mrs. Julie Jones, Mrs. Margaret Gwenlan, Mrs. Alison Moon, Mrs. Rhona Carlick (school clerk juniors), Mrs. Marian Whiteman (Deputy Head Ks2), Mrs. Patricia Wood (Head Teacher), Mrs. Heather Ryland (Deputy Head Ks1), Mrs. Ann Davies (school clerk infant dept), Mrs. Linda Williams, Mrs. Karen Jones.

213. Gelligaer Village School 1990s. Teacher Mrs. Gillian Fisher is seen with Thomas Summers, Andrew Kwiecinski, Nathan Lidster, David Exton, Anthony Lovis, Lucas Edwards, Stephen Crocker, Ceri-Anne Porter, Rhiannon Jones, Kylie Bell, Siobhan Thomas, Katherine Thomas, Adrianne Brown, Rhiannon Greenway, Abbie Crocker, Daniel King, Nikhaela King, Richard Cox, Amy Crocker, Thomas Williams, Rachel Jones, Daniel McCarthy, Gareth Dare, Shannon O'Halloran, Laura Cox, Jade Fisher, Laura Hayes, Zoe Hanson, Rachel Webb, Layton Jones.

214. The pupils of Gelligaer Village Infants School are seen here during the school's celebrations of the Queen's Golden Jubilee. The yard party was one of the day's events and it was something the children will never forget. There was plenty to eat with all the nice things you one could imagine; pop, crisps, and cakes, trifles all catered for by the staff of the school.

215. Greenhill Primary School late 1990s. Miss Kitchen (teacher), Iuan Edwards, Richard Davies, Mathew Jenkins, Richard Lewis, Jason Wild, Liam Morgan, Melvin Norman, Miss Jones (teacher). Demi Williams, Lindsay Ellis, Ceri-Anne Lanchbury, Chloe Goddard, Lorraine Edwards, James Kemp, Emma Hardcastle, Jessica Sayer, Joshua Jenkins, Rachel Selwood, James Shortman, Alan Davies, Amy Jenkins, Chelsea Wicks, Nathan Barry, Sarah Watkins, Catherine Johnson, Geraldine Jenkins, Gerwyn Martin, Lorraine Jones, Mathew Hilton.

216. Some of the pupils of Greenhill Primary School during the Queen's Golden Jubilee celebrations are seen here ready to let go their balloons in one of the events. The furthest distance recorded was by Ieuan Edwards and was found in Germany winning him a prize of £25. In the picture are Arron Davies, Luke Hilton, James Shortman, Emma Pope, Mathew Williams, Demi Williams, Natasha Pritchard, Zara Watkins, Rachel Selwood, Ceri-Anne Lanchbury, Richard Lewis, Lloyd Lewis, Jamie Cousins, Lauren Jones, Jessica Sayer, Lyndsay Ellis, Jamie Gillgrass, Ashley Jones, Joshua Rees, Ieuan Edwards.

217./218. Greenhill Primary School was opened in December 1969. A few years later the school opened its special needs unit for children with physical disabilities, this meant that physically handicapped children could now be educated along with their able bodied peers which had and has continued to have, a very positive impact on the school's ethos and the behaviour and attitude of all the children. In September 2001 the school opened a second special needs unit for children with social and communication difficulties. This has proved over the year to be equally as rewarding for the school. The school has continued over the years to go from strength to strength and was awarded an excellent Inspection Report in June 2001. To confirm the findings of the Inspectors in May 2002, the school was awarded the Basic Skills Quality Mark by the Basic Skills Agency. This award is for excellence in the teaching and learning of the basic skills of mathematics and English.

219. Big Pit miners Gelligaer Village Junior School Class 4A in March 1990. The 'miners' are Nicola Young, Emily Simmons, Glenn Shide, Dana Davies, Louise Jones, Eleanor Whiteman, Mrs. Marian Whiteman (teacher). Barri Hamer, Chris Lewis, Gareth Higgs, Gareth Reed, Ross Bethel, Marie Woods, Louise Lewis, Ceri Jayne.

220. Gelligaer Village School 1997 on St. Davids Day with Nathan Lidster, Rhiannon Greenaway, Shannon O'Halloran, Rhys Powell, Rhiann Rogers, Adrianne Brown, Stephen Crocker, Laura Constance, Stephen Moyle, Amy Crocker, Anthony Lovis, Catherine Davies, Kris Wilson, Cerianne Porter, Gerwyn Edwards, Joanne Porter, Gareth Dare, Thomas Summers, Laura Cox, Shane Marsh, Jaye Connelly, Luke Bishop, Carol-Anne Morgan, Mathew Farr, Rachel Jones, Andrew Parsons, Daniel Lewis, Zoe Hanson, Siobhan Thomas.

221. A delightful class of play-group children from the area is seen here in the vestry of Horeb Chapel in Gelligaer. The children of the area came to know it as Aunty Maureen's, and it gave them a good start to school days and learning to mix with others. In the picture are Maureen Puddyfoot, Janet ?, Julie Greenhouse, Joanne, James, Shaun, William, Louise, Abigail, Robert, Jennifer, Rhys, Gareth, Richard, and Richard, Natalie, Nerys, Joanne, Jason, Annette, Amy, Rebbeca.

222. Gilfach School in 1964. Pictured are Raymond Gardner, David Gallatin, Anne Payne, Susan James, Jocelyn Roberts, Janet Evans, Kathleen Clark, Julie Weaver, Mary Fletcher, Gary Shide, Keith Lewis, Clive Davies, Andrew Rees, Roger Allen, Kieran O'Hagan, Grant Davies, Tony Grisley, Ernie Woods, John Evans, Robert Lewis, Paul Harris, David Gwilym, Sandra Williams, Elizabeth Richards, Lorraine Lewis, Jane Payne, Ruth Sallis, Mrs. Watkins, Vida Guzvic, Janice Hill, Denise Baker, Diane Jenkins, Jane Smith, Mary Thomas, Susan Oliver, Diane Eaton, Hillary Lewis, Wendy Dando and Sheryl Dowler.

223. Gilfach School in the 1960s. Back standing Sylvia Walters, Jocelyn Parry, Lynne Williams, Gillian ?, Valerie Trew, Fiona Hopkins, Mrs. Wallace (Teacher). Forward Standing ?, David Lewis, Nigel Grant, Mark Williams, Jeannete Thomas, Helen Phillmore, Mark Davies, Jeremy ?, Brian Jenkins, Colin Trew, Ian Duncan. Seated Wendy ?, Elaine Angel, Barbara Lewis, Tina Palmer, ?, Gail Thomas, Linda Biddle, Linda Horrell, Katrina Williams. Front seated Kashmir Frazies, Michael Oliver, Michael Trivett, Chris Jennick, Gerald Jones.

224. Gilfach School in 1958. Top row: Raymond Hughes, Howard Llewellyn, William Thomas, Ceri Jones. Middle row: Derek Steed, Robert Davey, Richard Sallis, Russell ?, Alan Davies, ? Hopkins, Bret Stewart, John Walters, Mr. Anwel Jones, Bottom row: Alan Williams, Graham Lloyd, David Price, Tony Holt, Gerald Davies, Rhys Evans, Malcolm Beale, John Evans, Ray Powell.

225. Gilfach School in the 1960s. Back ?, Geoff Way, Lorraine Baker, Sheryl Edwards, Lorraine Short, ?, Ann Mathews, Robert Gemmell, Anthony Williams. Middle ?, Mark Rees, Garnet Price, Mark Evans, ?, ? Sallis, David Wall, ?, Phillip Johnson, Mark Griffiths, Anthony Lucas, Gary ?. Front Susan Willetts, ?, Dawn Fraser, Janice Short, Mrs. Jones (Teacher), Tina Tasker, Jennifer Pope, ?, Lorna Thomas.

226. Another look at Gilfach School in the 1950s with just the names of Mr. Anwel Jones, Alun Thomas, Billy Summers, Colin Williams, Alan Stevens.

227. Glanynant Primary School 1968. Teacher Mrs. Morris with Mandy Wilcox, Susan Fraser, ?, Mandy Hyatt, Michael Roberts, Andrew Richards, David Jones, Vince Price, ?, ?, Glen Jenkins, Shaun Edwards, ?, Catherine Adams, ?, ?, Margaret Duncan, Alison Probert, Lesley Derrick.

228. St. David's Day at Glanynant Primary School 1978. Craig Marshall, Kalwyn Thomas, ?, Paul Darch, ?, Martin Butts, Paul Jones, Mark Bridgway, Emma ?, Debbie Jones, Rachel Loughton, Rhianon Greening, ?, Nadine ?, Ann Marie Price, Hayley Thomas, Rhian Watkins, Nicola Dawson, Nicola Warburton, Carol Hobbs, Natalie Price, Wayne Pope.

229. St. David's Day at Gelligaer School 1964-65 and included in the picture are girls from some of the classes. Denise Lewis, Lyn Owen, Meryl Gorham, Julie Marsden, Jackie Marsden, Adie Corns, Sheryl Rowlands, Pauline Haydn, Annette Lewis, Angela McCarthy, Rita Ackerman, Gloria Gilbert, Susan Davies, Janette Holder, Kathryn Benson, Miriam Greening, Ann Jenkins, Susan Bray, Sheila Rowlands, Catherine Thomas, Pamela Lewis, Susan Gillard and Julie Rogers.

230. Glan-y-Nant School in the early 1970s. The young ladies pictured include Ann Whitcombe, Beverley Williams, Lynette Thomas, Eryl Thomas, Ceri Gingell, Kathryn Watkins, Gaynor Jenkins, Kathryn Adams, Kathleen Higgins, Lynda Thomas. Second row: Alison Probert, Lesley Derrick. Front: Jane Angel, Lorraine Davey, Andrea Harding, Lynne Jones, Louise Probert, Lynne Chandler, Jane Lewis and Ceri Lewis.

Acknowledgements

Sincere thanks are due to the following who kindly loaned some of their material for inclusion in this book and apologies are offered to anyone whose name has been omitted inadvertently.

Brian and Lillian Adams, Mrs. G. Anstice, Vince Alan, Granville Boyland, Bernice Bampfield, Bargoed Library, Beechgrove Social Club, Mrs. Bray, Peter Bennett (Maritime and Industrial Museum), Nigel and Celia Brake, Arthur Callow, Sheryl Cartwright, Peter Carter, Caerphilly County Borough Councils Museums and Heritage Service, Sid Carter, Tresa Cox, Pat Clabby, Michael Cushion, Keith Derrick, John Dimes, Ann Davies, Ken Davey, Ian Duncan, Dai and Maureen Edwards, Nan Exton, Robert Evans, Iris Evans, Carol Evans, Joyce Evans, Graham Fewins, Chris Griffin, Gelligaer Boxing Club, Gelligaer Village School, Gelligaer Bowls, Greenhill School, Elaine Harris, Keith Harris, Alison Greenaway, Karen Goddard, Molly Holder, Janet and Gareth Hopkins, Tommy Haywood, Phyllis Horrell, Lyn James, Barbara Jennick, Glen Jenkins, Paul James, Graham Jones, K. Jones, Mrs. Kitt, Adele Lockyear, Jean Lewer, Glyn Lucas, Phillip Lee, Jean Lewis, J. Lynch, Jane Marlow, Pat and Fay Murphy, Alan Morgan, Yvonne Martin, Chris Morgan, Liz M'Que, Photographic Archive National Museum of Welsh Life, Mrs. Partridge, Mrs. Phillimore, John and Marilyn Probert, Maureen Puddyfoot, Lynda Paynter, David Price, Glenys Parker, Brian Porter, T. Pritchard, Mr. Pritchard, Robert Quirk, Brian Reynolds, Denise Rees, Emlyn Richards, Mostyn Richards, Allan and Ceridwen Rogers, Vi Stevens, Jim and Sue Stephens, Rosalyn Sage, Pat Sage, Duncan Stonelake, Dino Spinetti, Dave Thomas, Megan Thomas, Glyn Thomas, Jim Thomson, Mike Thomas, John Wood, Glyn Whitcombe, Jennifer Williams, Marian Whiteman, Ystrad Mynach Library.

Also available by the same authors:

Ystrad Mynach

including Hengoed, Cefn Hengoed and Maesycwmmer

in Photographs

- Volume 1

214 Black & White photographs covering the 4 areas.

ISBN 1 874538 39 5

Available from bookshops or from Old Bakehouse Publications Tel: 01495 212600

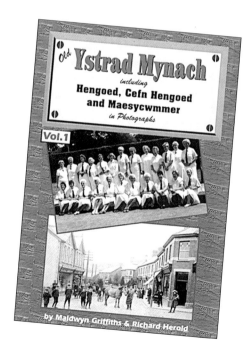